POWER & PASSION

SIX CHARACTERS IN SEARCH OF RESURRECTION

POWER & PASSION

SIX CHARACTERS IN & SEARCH OF RESURRECTION

SAMUEL WELLS

ZONDERVAN®

GRAND RAPIDS, MICHIGAN 49530 USA

ZONDERVAN.COM/
AUTHORTRACKER

We want to hear from you. Please send your comments about this book to us in care of zreview@zondervan.com. Thank you.

ZONDERVAN®

Power and Passion
Copyright © 2007 by Samuel Wells

Requests for information should be addressed to:
Zondervan, *Grand Rapids, Michigan 49530*

Library of Congress Cataloging-in-Publication Data

Wells, Samuel, 1965 –
    Power and passion : six characters in search of Resurrection / Samuel Wells.
        p.   cm.
    ISBN-13: 978-0-310-27017-1
    ISBN-10: 0-310-27017-0
    1. Holy Week. 2. Jesus Christ—Passion. 3. Bible. N.T. Gospels—
Biography. I. Title.
    BT414.W45 2006
    242'.35—dc22

                                                                            2006022095

Interior design by Beth Shagene

Printed in the United Kingdom

---

06 07 08 09 10 11 12 • 18 17 16 15 14 13 12 11 10 9 8 7 6 5 4 3 2 1

To the people of St Mark's, Newnham, Cambridge

CONTENTS

Foreword by the Archbishop of Canterbury   9

Acknowledgments   11

Introduction   13

1. Pontius Pilate   25

2. Barabbas   55

3. Joseph of Arimathea   85

4. Mrs Pilate   109

5. Peter   133

6. Mary Magdalene   159

A Note on Sources and Further Reading   189

Notes   192

FOREWORD

Christian reflection, when it is really doing its job, is about making connections between unlikely partners – as Jesus himself made the supremely radical connections between heaven and earth, purity and sin, divinity and humanity. Sam Wells, in this searching and direct book, asks us to think about the connections between passion and politics. Passion is something we think of chiefly in terms of personal intensity; politics is about managing things and calculating possibilities, and so – as often as not – compromising that intensity. But what if they do belong together in a way that makes passion more than a recipe for mere gestures, and politics more than a round of rather shabby horse-trading?

Sam Wells argues that if we look at how the gospel stories of the passion of Jesus understand power and conflict, we learn something essential about connecting politics and passion. We learn about recognizing the power we have – and about our frequent reluctance to do so and our desire to present ourselves as victims of circumstances. We learn about the mistakes we can make in trying to identify the forces that make for change and about how Jesus changes the very definition of change. We learn about what might be involved in fully owning the faith that shapes us and motivates us; about the unexpected role of those who don't profess the kind of faith we instantly recognize; about the tensions for Christian leaders between individual discipleship and effective responsibility for others. And finally we are brought to a vision of friendship and forgiveness as the very center of a transformed set of political possibilities.

I said earlier that this is a searching book, and so it is. It drives the reader back into asking himself or herself some pretty hard questions, and in doing that, it brings us face-to-face with Jesus in a rare way. The opportunities for reflection at the end of every chapter, however, have nothing confrontational about them. They are carefully and compassionately designed invitations to growth in faith and maturity.

Sam Wells is an outstanding thinker and an outstanding pastor. This Lent book is a distillation of real wisdom – and passion as well, passion that is channelled lovingly and thoughtfully toward the health of church and world. I have found reading it to be indeed an encounter with the crucified and risen Jesus, and I hope all of its other readers will find the same.

– DR ROWAN WILLIAMS
ARCHBISHOP OF CANTERBURY

ACKNOWLEDGMENTS

I am deeply grateful to Archbishop Rowan for the invitation to write this book. It has been an honor and a delight. Archbishop Rowan's wisdom, generosity, and grace have been an inspiration to me for many years.

I wish to thank those who have shared the formation of this project as it has emerged. I am especially conscious of John Kiess, who helped me find the words, Jo Bailey Wells, who helped me find the time, and my colleagues at Duke University Chapel and at Duke Divinity School, who helped me find the space. Several people kindly read parts or all of the manuscript and knocked off some of its corners: Lauren Winner, Stanley Hauerwas, Janet Scovil, Ana Ponce, and Jennifer Lawson.

I wrote this book shortly after moving from Cambridge, England, to Durham, North Carolina. It seemed an appropriate moment to think about power. The church in the American South appears to have the things the church in England most laments its lack of: numbers, money, and social influence. I have not noticed that having these attributes makes the life of the Christian faith more straightforward. But I am acutely aware that from those to whom much is given, much will be expected. This is therefore an initial attempt to describe how Christians may engage with their own power and thus begin to meet some of those expectations.

One deep regret on leaving England was to leave behind the people of St Mark's, Newnham. One cannot always perceive the image of the reign of God through the prism of the local church, but sometimes one has a sense that clarity is emerging. It was therefore with mixed feelings that I said goodbye to a place and a people who had shown me so much of what God is about. One particular experience I shall never forget was the performance of the twelve plays in Dorothy L. Sayers's cycle of Jesus' ministry, *The Man Born to Be King.* To my 100 colleagues among the troupe of sometimes unlikely actors, to Marguerite Roberts and those many others among the participating audience of 2,000, and to Rex Walford and those others who conceived and produced the event, I owe so much – not least the idea for chapters 3 and 4 of this book. I am also indebted to Jeremy Begbie for the idea that gave rise to chapter 5.

I left St Mark's without receiving all I had to receive, and without giving all I had to give. I hope this book will be a token of what I did receive, and of what I hope, in a different way, I still have to give.

INTRODUCTION

WHAT THIS BOOK IS SEEKING TO DO

I believe that in Jesus' resurrection lies the power to transform the passion of our lives. This transformed passion gives disciples a new power that is best described as a new politics because it changes so many of the things we take for granted about what makes the world go round.

I have four broad aims in writing this book.

The first is to renew readers in a life of humble, faithful, sometimes sacrificial, but deeply joyful Christian discipleship. This book should draw the reader to repentance, empowerment, and encouragement. *Repentance*, as it explores the way our lives are profoundly shaped by notions of power that run counter to the power of God and are in the grip of passions that withdraw us from the transforming passion of God offered in Christ. *Empowerment*, as the reader sees where true power lies and in what true passion consists – and as the book explores the kinds of practices and gestures that embody the power and passion made possible in Christ. And *encouragement*, as it points unambiguously toward Easter as the focus of true power and true passion, demonstrating how God has given us, in the resurrection of Jesus Christ, the gifts we need to live a passionate life beyond the fear of death.

Repentance, empowerment, and encouragement are the heart of the Christian tradition of Lent. Forty days were set aside to prepare catechumens for baptism at the Easter vigil. During these forty days, new Christians would pray, fast, read the Bible, share their faith, give alms, and examine their hearts. These practices shaped them in repentance, empowered them for discipleship, and encouraged them in faith. I hope reading this book will do the same for Christians who seek repentance, empowerment, and encouragement today.

The second aim of the book is to renew the excitement of Christians at the wonderful gift God has given us in the Bible. Two kinds of Bible readers shout loudest at present. One sees the Bible as a series of legal guidelines, handed down in an apparently arbitrary way by what seems to be a rather culturally distant God. The Bible appears to offer a rather constrained life, with plenty of prohibitions, but one that is claimed to be good for us in the end, certainly as far as eternal salvation is concerned. The problem with this rather constrained view of the Bible is its understanding of God as a mysterious judge with unfathomable expectations who is always likely to catch his people out. The second noisy kind of Bible reader sees the Bible as a series of noble injunctions, largely about setting people free or affirming them as they are; the details get rather lost in the urge to generalize God's affirmation of humanity and his desire for flourishing life. The problem with this way of reading the Bible is that it calls into question why one would read the Bible at all, since it tells us little that has not already been well expressed by the poets, storytellers, and social prophets of every age. God tends to become invisible behind a cloud of abstract goals such as justice, peace, and love.

I set out in this book to renew a sense that the Bible gives Christians something that is not available elsewhere, empowering them for engagement with the world in the Spirit of Jesus Christ. My strategy is to pay attention to the details of the Passiontide story, details that are invariably overlooked in the rush to get to the cross. By highlighting six characters from the Holy Week narratives, I am offering a different way of engaging with the cross of Christ. I want the reader to see how much is in the detail of the story. The story is not simply a means to an end, a series of historical footnotes to a rigid logic of "why the Son of God had to die to save us". Instead, the story offers us a series of alternative ways of following (or not following) Jesus and a series of encounters (conscious or unconscious) with the living God. The characters in the Holy Week narrative face choices and experience feelings very similar to our own. We should therefore read their stories expecting that each detail may have a bearing on our path in Jesus' footsteps.

The third motivation behind this book is to help readers realize their own power. Looking over my years in ministry, I reflect that this has been a consistent theme of my preaching, counsel, and writing. I have sought to help people in a working-class town discover the power they could find in their unity as the body of Christ and become a thriving community of hope in a neighborhood losing its identity historically rooted in heavy industry. I have tried to inspire people on a socially disadvantaged housing estate to realize that, like the beleaguered congregations to whom Paul wrote, they had the elixir of new life in Christ, regardless of the mockery and hostility and indifference of most of their neighbors. I have endeavored to encourage people in more affluent suburbs to see their true identity in the practices and disciplines of the church and to see life not so much as an individual project as a corporate program for holy living. And now I preach to a very large congregation in one of the most influential institutions in the United States, and still I sense the need to dispel an abiding sense of powerlessness among those who gather for worship and to help them discover their power – in God and, when united, in the church.

People seldom acknowledge their power but find it easier to articulate their passion. I aim in this book to engage with the reader's passion, but to help the reader see how that passion is shaped by assumptions about power. I suggest that this is exactly what the gospel accounts of Christ's death and resurrection are about, and I seek to show that they offer us a new kind of passion based on a transformed understanding of power. I hope that the reader will emerge with as strong an understanding of their own power – given to them by what God has done in Christ – as they previously had of their own passion.

And the final motivation for writing this book is that I once read a book that transformed my understanding of the relation-ship between Jesus' life and the way I live my life today. It was called *The Politics of Jesus* and was published in 1972 by the late Mennonite theologian John Howard Yoder. I simply want to give the reader of this book the experience I had in reading that one. Yoder takes each of the conventional reasons for assuming Jesus is irrelevant to the practical and profound matters of power and passion in our lives and dismantles them one by one. Jesus (it is said) assumed he was speaking about a short interim period that would be abruptly concluded by a cataclysmic end of the world. Or, Jesus was a simple rural figure concerned only with face-to-face relations. Or, Jesus was released from any genuine social responsibility because he was always going to be a member of a small minority far removed from the circles of power that Chris-tians today must negotiate in ways he did not anticipate. Or, Jesus was interested in spiritual, not social, matters; he was concerned not with political change but with a new self-understanding. Or,

Jesus came simply to give his life for the sins of humankind, and the kind of life he led beforehand only illustrates the sinlessness of the sacrificial victim he became.

But what if, Yoder asks, these views of Jesus are all ways of avoiding the simple assumption that Jesus is the template for the power and passion of our lives? What if we are called to follow Jesus in one specific respect above all others: his willingness to walk the way of the cross in contrast to the host of political and social alternatives available to him? This book seeks to take up Yoder's mantle and begin with the same assumption. It seeks to describe six political alternatives available to Jesus – and, broadly, to us – and to portray the power and passion of Jesus in the light of them, in such a way that the nature of the power and the direction of the passion available to us become transparent.

WHAT THIS BOOK ASSUMES

This book makes five assumptions. It may be helpful to explain them at the outset.

I assume that the Gospels were intended to be pondered, word by word, action by action, scene by scene, by communities seeking to embody their faith in Jesus in practical acts of discipleship in the world. I vividly recall an occasion when I participated in a corporate meditation on a passage from John's gospel, in a style sometimes known as *lectio divina*. Around twenty-five people were present. The passage was read, and we meditated in silence on significant words or phrases. The passage was read again, and we spoke aloud words or phrases that had spoken to us. The passage was read a third time, and we spoke aloud meanings that we had never perceived before. And it dawned on me that this was how John's gospel was written. A community treasured and read aloud stories and sayings that had been handed down from participants in Jesus' ministry. And the community deeply pondered these traditions and tried to embody them in their discipleship. And eventually they were written down, with deep-layered significance given to each treasured word.

And this is why I believe it is quite legitimate to seek in the Gospels the kinds of meanings I draw out in these chapters. It is not just legitimate – it is expected, required even. When one accepts that the communities from which these documents emerged had the highest possible understanding of the humanity and divinity of Christ and thus the deepest imaginable commitment to nurturing and revering the words written and remembered about him, one loses the fear of "overinterpreting" the text. That does not mean all interpretations are equally helpful, but one must also remember that there is no such thing as a "plain" reading that is not already an interpretation. To suppose, for example, that the Gospels are quasi-journalistic accounts concerned only with broad historical accuracy as perceived by an eyewitness, or to presume that the Gospels are uninterested in the resonances of events and words that emerged only after long percolating in worshiping communities, would be to make huge and very questionable assumptions. Every reader must choose how much and what kind of information to regard as relevant. For example, every reader must decide to what extent to try to harmonize disparities in the gospel accounts of similar incidents such as the anointing of Jesus, or whether to consult other documents of the period for accounts of well-attested historical figures such as Pontius Pilate. The test of which readings prove fruitful simply emerges through the experience, wisdom, and grace of the Spirit working in the church over time. There is no shortcut to a single "correct" reading nor any guarantee that there can be a reading that has found everything the text offers to every person in every culture in every time. God continues to bring forth grace from his holy Word.

My second assumption is that some parts of the Gospels have a special significance, even within texts that are themselves unique in their importance for Christians. I refer to the accounts of the passion, death, and resurrection of Jesus. Mark's gospel is sometimes called a passion narrative with a long introduction. All the gospel writers seem to assume that Jesus' death and resurrection are the hinge of history, that nothing that was true before can ever be assumed to be the same again, and that nothing that was considered impossible before need necessarily be assumed to be impossible after. In short, all bets are off. The season of Lent usually begins with a consideration of the disciplines of the body and the schooling of desire, often with a consideration of Christ's temptations in the desert. But before long, it changes gear and heads with Jesus toward Jerusalem, taking up the way of the cross. In this study, I have concentrated on some of the details of the key moments in Jerusalem – those few days that changed the direction of human destiny. I am assuming that every single character mentioned in the narrative is there for a reason. Even Pontius Pilate's wife, who appears in only one verse, has a vital role to play. These are events whose significance it is impossible to overestimate. No detail is trivial. Jesus had many alternatives available to him; he chose the way of the cross. It is central to the life of the church and every Christian to meditate deeply on why he made that choice and on what that choice means for following him today.

Third, I assume that Christians are, and always have been, in the business of politics. Christianity has no withdrawn "spiritual" realm aloof from "worldly" politics. Politics is a day-to-day matter for every person, not a specialist subject for the argumentative and opinionated, or a dirty business for the manipulative or unfortunate. Politics is not an inappropriate intrusion into a spiritual conversation, nor is it an introduction of unnecessary controversy into an otherwise harmonious discourse. Politics is the careful negotiation of passion and interest that pays due respect to different degrees and kinds of power. In other words, broadly understood, politics is a dimension of every interaction, from a parent encouraging a child to share, to a group of housekeepers demanding a minimum wage, to a superpower trying to limit the proliferation of nuclear weapons in the developing world. As is often said, everything is politics, but politics is not everything. As soon as one acknowledges that everyone has passion, that everyone has a degree of power, and that everyone has something to gain and something to lose from a change in the status quo, one has accepted that politics is part of every aspect of life.

And the gospel of Jesus Christ is deeply concerned with how individuals and groups use their power, how they form their passions, and how society is going to change radically. It is not a question of getting involved in politics; everyone already is. It is more a question of becoming wiser and more conscious and more faithful in one's politics. The only Christians who say we should keep politics and the gospel apart are those who enjoy a comfortable social and economic status and assume the point of Christianity is to underwrite the privileges they already have.

My fourth assumption is that power is not necessarily a bad thing. There is a strand in Christian spirituality that emphasizes the humility of Jesus, the way he spent his life with the sick and the poor, and the way he was rejected by the religious and political leaders of his day, and it assumes that power is something Jesus renounced. This mistakenly assumes that there is only one kind of power. My aim in this book is to show that there are several kinds of power – that property, prestige, and military force must be set alongside other dynamics such as sexual power and friendship – and that none of these has anything to compare with God's power, which is the power of creation and, ultimately and definitively, of resurrection. The power based on property and control of resources presupposes a world of scarcity where there is never enough – never enough food, never enough wisdom, never enough time, and, deep down, never enough God. The power based on resurrection is a power presupposing abundance – plenty of life, and therefore plenty of time, of gifts, of companions, of revelation, of forgiveness – and an overwhelming plenty of God.

Fundamentally the transformation of politics is about the transformation of the reality – and perception – of power. The politics that knows no resurrection, which I describe in the first three chapters of this book, is a politics of scarcity, concerning the more or less violent debate over the more or less just distribution of inevitably limited resources. The politics of resurrection, which emerges in the final two chapters, is a politics of abundance, concerning the joyful deliberation over the best use of the plenteous gifts of God. This book seeks to show how Jesus' resurrection introduces the politics of abundance by transforming the reality of power.

And my final assumption is that passion is the heart of the gospel. I am deliberately playing with more than one understanding of passion. In the narrowest sense, *the passion* is the traditional term for the period of voluntary suffering Jesus endured as he went to the cross. It is the subject of almost limitless reflection and devotion in striking art, sweeping music, provocative drama, grand liturgy, and humble prayer. This is a book about the passion, seen from the point of view of the minor characters and with particular attention to their power and to the politics of the events. But more generally, *passion* refers to a heartfelt and overwhelming longing, a profound and sometimes crazy love, usually, though not always, for something or someone just out of reach. I am assuming this is a phenomenon the reader of this book can relate to, indeed has experienced or is experiencing. Perhaps the reader needs permission to name and explore that passion. This book is a call to recognize that passion is the heart of politics and the heart of faith.

There is an underlying sense that passion has an abiding erotic dimension – that the word *passion* conjures up images of desperate figures like Catherine and Heathcliff, braving the wind and the moors and their own tragic mistakes in Emily Brontë's novel *Wuthering Heights*, or of the desperate love of the rich Rose and the poor and dying Jack amid the sinking wreck of the doomed ship in the film *Titanic*. This book does not seek to downplay this dimension of passion but instead seeks to show how the power of resurrection transforms the doomed character of passion.

The book assumes that all passion, whether conscious or not, is a more or less adequate form of passion for God. And further, all passion for God is a more or less adequate analogy for the passion that really matters, the passion that drives the transformation of cross and resurrection – God's passion for us. God's longing for us led him to take on in Christ voluntary suffering that expressed his love. But that suffering and death were transformed in a way no passion has been before. In resurrection passion changed the nature of power from control over limited life to access to unlimited life. In so doing, it transformed the potential of passion from the epitome of hopeless gestures in the face of finitude to a glorious anticipation of God's way of salvation. For in the end, the repentance, empowerment, and encouragement offered by this book come down to one question. We are God's passion; is he ours?

HOW TO READ THIS BOOK

I have written this book in such a way that the argument builds momentum as it goes along. But I have also tried to shape the book in such a way that each chapter can be read on its own, perhaps for a weekly discussion, or a chapter can indeed be missed out altogether, without losing the thread of the argument, should it not be possible to read the whole book. For those who like to read their books from back to front, the conclusion of the final chapter offers a summary of the argument.

A group is an ideal setting for reading this book. I see the flourishing of book groups as a secular mimicking of the Christian practice of fellowship house-groups and small-group Bible studies. Such a group shares the intimacy of reading with the insight of faith and the challenge of a common call to discipleship. That is exactly the culture in which I would imagine this book being best heard and understood. One cannot talk about passion and politics without being personal, being anecdotal, being compassionate, and planning for change at the same time, and that is what groups do best.

One feature that may or may not be familiar to readers is the way each chapter ends. I have offered a number of "wonderings" to stimulate responses, meditations, sharing, explorations, or further wonderings. Wonderings are not questions. They have a full stop at the end, not a question mark. To address them, one has to leave aside the determination to get the right answer and instead has to open oneself to responses that invite further engagement. It is like the difference between a soccer match, in which the object is to score a goal, and the warm-up beforehand, when players gently scoop the ball up to one another, trying as a circle to keep the ball in the air. Wondering is more like the soccer players' warm-up, a way of shaping one's insights so as to be upbuilding to the group. It is not about showing how clever one is or about how many commentaries one has read or about setting companions straight about the "correct" interpretation. Wondering is particularly inclusive of those of tender years or with fewer recognized accomplishments, who may well find it easier to engage their imaginations in a suitably unconstrained way.

The wonderings are not integral to the chapters, and groups or individual readers must feel at liberty to ignore them. But I offer them out of many years' experience of discovering God's gift of Scripture more deeply with adults and children through the activity of Godly Play, a method of exploring Christian faith rooted in the Montessori tradition. Through Godly Play, and especially through the corporate wondering that is at the heart of it, I have come to value the gentle probing of the imagination as a vital way of hearing everything God has to give us through his Word and of uniting Bible study with prayer.

At the conclusion of each chapter comes a prayer that may be said at the end of a group meeting or by an individual in quiet devotion. I have chosen to conclude with a prayer for two related reasons. One is that when Christians say the Creed together, they do so in the form of a prayer that begins "We believe" and ends with the word "Amen". This teaches us that all our knowledge and understanding is, fundamentally, a prayer. Hence the activity of reading this book will be a form of prayer. Second, I am deeply grateful to those who persuaded me five or six years ago that part of the ministry to which God had called me was to write books. Since then books have poured out of me, largely because I have found that writing is the way I most easily pray. In seeking to formulate truth in words, I search deep into the heart of the God of Jesus Christ in a way others do in silence or service or solitude. Including a formal prayer in each chapter is a simple way of drawing attention to the fact that the whole enterprise of theological exploration is, for me, a prayer. I hope sharing my discovery will encourage others to find their distinctive gifts in prayer.

May this book be a prayer that God's people find their passion transformed in a new politics made possible by the power of Jesus' resurrection.

CHAPTER 1

PONTIUS PILATE

Pontius Pilate is usually portrayed as an honest broker surrounded by fanatical hotheads. This portrayal is not based on what the gospel accounts tell us about Pilate. The Roman governor had a strong, vested interest in the outcome of Jesus' trial. Although the gospel writers portray Pilate's character and interests differently, they each give us a vivid picture of the alliances that closed in on Jesus.

People with executive power often like to see themselves as honest brokers. But power is a gift and is principally given for setting people free. Most of us have a great deal more power than we realize. We too can try to hide behind the ambiguities of public responsibility or the pretense that we have no vested interests. This chapter considers the nature of political power and the possibilities of the power we each have.

ROME AND THE MANIPULATION OF POWER

Rome dominated the Mediterranean world and many territories far beyond. The key source of wealth was land, and the Roman aristocracy was largely made up of great landowners.

These landowners controlled the rest of the population of the empire through military force, tax collection, and a patronage network that assumed the extortion of bribes. Judea was no different. To understand the political dynamics of the four gospel accounts, one needs to place the events of the story between these controlling forces: soldiers, tax gatherers, and quislings (those in the governor's "pocket"). Among the first category we find the centurion whose servant Jesus healed; among the second category we find Matthew the disciple and Zacchaeus; among the third category we find Herod Antipas, Caiaphas, and Nicodemus.

The gospel accounts of Jesus' birth and death can be somewhat confusing because of the number of different people who seem to be in charge. For example, when Pilate discovers Jesus is from Galilee, a region that was not directly ruled by Rome, he sends Jesus to Herod Antipas, the vassal ruler of that region (Luke 23.5–12). Later, the Jerusalem authorities (whom John's gospel confusingly and disturbingly calls "the Jews"), having condemned Jesus, need the Roman governor's authority to make this a death sentence. Pilate says to these so-called leaders, "Here is your king" – whereupon they respond, "We have no king but Caesar" (John 19.14–15).

This demeaning state of affairs is due to the manner in which the Roman emperor ran his empire. Rather than dominate and overrun his subject people, he creamed off perhaps 5 percent of the population to act as retainers. These people would get significant benefits in terms of the three most important things: wealth, prestige, and power. All that was required in return was loyalty to Rome. Thus at the time of Jesus' birth, Rome could afford not to rule Judea directly. Instead, it simply controlled the people and raised taxes through a vassal king, Herod the Great. But Herod died shortly after Jesus was born, and his sons had neither his authority nor his skill. So following Herod's death, Rome took to administering the province directly, by installing a governor.

Nonetheless, they kept on the various hierarchies of retainers to act as intermediaries between them and the largely Jewish population. And well they might, for as some who are used to being in charge are fond of saying, "Why keep dogs and bark yourself?" Pilate and his predecessors had found a formula that meant they could control the province and meanwhile acquire considerable wealth for themselves, not by suppressing the people with military force but by manipulating those among the population who sought the three things that really mattered in the Roman Empire: wealth, prestige, and power. That is why in the Gospels there are only occasional encounters and confrontations with Roman authorities and soldiers. Most of the disputes are with Rome's stooges – those whose obedience to Rome demonstrated they had lost all sight of being God's holy people.

The most interesting aspects in a society are those things that everyone takes for granted. Pontius Pilate is a significant figure, even before one considers his role in relation to Jesus' death, because he had achieved everything that his culture most valued. Pontius Pilate's parents would have been members of the Roman aristocracy among the equestrian class – in other words, rich and influential but not quite senator material. We could call them knights rather than lords. These knights used their class advantages to gain wealth, prestige, and power. The equestrian class generally served the empire in military office; if they succeeded, they could end up becoming a prefect of one of the more troublesome provinces. Judea was one of those provinces. In AD 26, Pontius Pilate became its fifth prefect, or governor. His parents would have been very proud.

So the stage is set in Jerusalem: on the one hand stand the Jerusalem authorities, apparently manipulating the institutions of power but in practice in the pocket of the governor; and on the other hand Pontius Pilate, doing very well out of keeping the status quo and happy to let the Jerusalem authorities have a visible role in running the show. Enter Jesus of Nazareth at Passover. His presence was an issue that the Jerusalem authorities could not handle by themselves. He was not just a threat to the system of patronage and the manipulation of the elite; he was a threat to the Roman governor himself. Jesus not only emerged as a potential king, but he also undermined the dominant notions of wealth, prestige, and power and loosened their hold on the popular imagination. That was why it was inevitable that Jesus and Pilate would come face-to-face.

JESUS MEETS PILATE

Each of the Gospels offers a different slant on the meeting of Jesus and Pilate, and it is important to attend to the features of each narrative. (I shall not consider Mark's account explicitly, since it is almost entirely included in Matthew's account.)

Matthew

Matthew's gospel as a whole offers an extended study in how Jesus' teaching and ministry threaten the domination of the Jerusalem elites. The Jerusalem authorities are at Herod's side when he decides to wipe out the babes of Bethlehem (2.3 – 18); they seem to have as much to lose from the birth of a new king as Herod does. Later, they decide to kill Jesus (12.14) after he has perceived that the crowds have no adequate leaders (9.36). And the antagonism is not just on the side of the authorities. Jesus gives them every reason to hate him. He unambiguously denies that they represent God and calls them "blind guides" (15.14) before attacking the heart of their power. He claims they have transformed worship into profiteering and have kept their grip on the people by manipulating the temple taxes (21.12–13). He compares them to tenants who have betrayed their master (21.33–46), criticizes them as hypocrites and oppressors of the people, and finally announces that the temple, the center of their power, will be destroyed (24.2). The Jerusalem authorities and Jesus are on a collision course from the word go.

So it comes as no surprise that the Jerusalem authorities arrest and quickly condemn Jesus (26.57–68; 27.1–2). It is telling that Matthew records Judas's suicide before Jesus has even reached Pilate. This suggests that Judas recognized the Jerusalem elite and Pilate as being hand in glove with one another: Jesus' death was now inevitable. This is a sobering introduction to the conversation between Pilate and Jesus. The outcome is not in the balance; it is already settled. There is no question of casting Jesus as good, the authorities as bad, and Pilate as a vacillating middle man. The popular view of Pilate as a man of reason manipulated by a bunch of fanatics is not Matthew's view. Pilate will do whatever it takes to maintain his stranglehold on Judea, and there is no reason whatsoever to alienate his chief allies. Judas is correct in realizing that Jesus is already doomed.

Pilate's interaction with Jesus comes in three overlapping scenes.

1. Pilate Questions Jesus

Meanwhile Jesus stood before the governor, and the governor asked him, "Are you the king of the Jews?" "You have said so," Jesus replied. When he was accused by the chief priests and the elders, he gave no answer. Then Pilate asked him, "Don't you hear the testimony they are bringing against you?" But Jesus made no reply, not even to a single charge – to the great amazement of the governor. (27.11 – 14)

Here is an explicit confrontation between two rulers. Matthew calls Pilate "the governor" at this point, to emphasize the contrast. The simple question is, "Are you the king of the Jews?" What the question means is, "Do you set yourself up as the leader of this people in defiance of the Roman Emperor, in defiance of me, and in defiance of the Jerusalem authorities?" A whole sequence of figures in the first century – Simon, Athronges, Menachem, and a second Simon – did exactly this, and each of them was rubbed out by emperor, governor, or local elite.

Jesus is not a conventional king. He subverts the Roman assumption that what matters is wealth, status, and power. He has no use for wealth. He says, "No one can serve two masters" (6.24). Instead, he points out how rich one is if one trusts in God; he points out how even Solomon in all his wealth was not clothed like the lilies of the field – yet God will clothe his people much more extravagantly than the grass of the field. Therefore, he says, "Seek first his kingdom and his righteousness, and all these things will be given to you as well" (6.33). He subverts conventional notions of status. He says, "You know that the rulers of the Gentiles lord it over them, . . . Not so with you. Instead, whoever wants to become great among you must be your servant . . . just as the Son of Man did not come to be served, but to serve" (20.25 – 28). And he has no use for power, at least understood in the Roman sense as power backed by force. He rides into Jerusalem on a donkey with palm branches rather than on a horse with weapons and booty (21.1 – 11). He says, "Do not resist an evil person" (5.39), and even at the moment of his arrest he warns, "All who draw the sword will die by the sword" (26.52).

But Jesus is still a king. He stays silent before Pilate, perhaps echoing the words of Isaiah 53.7, "He was oppressed and afflicted, yet he did not open his mouth." But there is no reason for Pilate to doubt that Jesus is a king and thus a threat to Rome.

2. Pilate Consults the Crowd

Now it was the governor's custom at the Festival to release a prisoner chosen by the crowd. At that time they had a well-known prisoner whose name was Jesus Barabbas. So when the crowd had gathered, Pilate asked them, "Which one do you want me to release to you: Jesus Barabbas, or Jesus who is called the Messiah?" For he knew it was out of envy that they had handed Jesus over to him. While Pilate was sitting on the judge's seat, his wife sent him this message: "Don't have anything to do with that innocent man, for I have suffered a great deal today in a dream because of him." But the chief priests and the elders persuaded the crowd to ask for Barabbas and to have Jesus executed. "Which of the two do you want me to release to you?" asked the governor. "Barabbas," they answered. "What shall I do, then, with Jesus who is called the Messiah?" Pilate asked. They all answered, "Crucify him!" "Why? What crime has he committed?" asked Pilate. But they shouted all the louder, "Crucify him!" (27.15–23)

Here is a choice between two prisoners – Jesus Barabbas and Jesus called the Messiah. This scene undermines any reading of the story that paints Pilate as the evenhanded agent of justice. For justice is an early casualty of the whim of public opinion.

The choice, and the fact that both prisoners have the same name, Jesus ("Savior"), highlights the meaning of the title "Messiah". Messiah means "King of the Jews" – and King of the Jews means a challenge to Jerusalem and Rome. It is common today to regard politics and religion as largely separate spheres of influence, and certainly of authority. But such a distinction meant nothing to Caiaphas, who saw himself as leader of the people in his role as high priest, and it is not clear that it meant much to Jesus either. When Jesus says to Caiaphas, "You will see the Son of Man sitting at the right hand of the Mighty One and coming on the clouds of heaven" (26.64), it is pretty clear that the days of the cozy collusion between Caiaphas and Pilate are numbered.

Pilate sees that the Jerusalem authorities are jealous of Jesus, but his bread is buttered on the Jerusalem authorities' side, and he adeptly manipulates the crowd to ensure that Rome continues to appear as benefactor and is never revealed as oppressor.

3. Pilate Washes His Hands

When Pilate saw that he was getting nowhere, but that instead an uproar was starting, he took water and washed his hands in front of the crowd. "I am innocent of this man's blood," he said. "It is your responsibility!" All the people answered, "His blood is on us and on our children!" Then he released Barabbas to them. But he had Jesus flogged, and handed him over to be crucified. (27.24–26)

This concludes a masterful passage of political activity by Pilate. Not only does he dispose of a threat to his power system, but he also manages to get those most oppressed by the system ("all the people") to proclaim that the execution is their responsibility. His true motives are revealed when he has Jesus flogged before handing him over to be crucified – hardly the act of a reluctant fair-dealer.

The first scene brought together Pilate the governor and Jesus the king. In the second scene the contrast was between Barabbas the savior and Jesus the savior. Here now in the third scene is the most ironic contrast: Pilate, who presents his actions to the people as "innocent" and "for you", and Jesus, whose death points out Pilate's guilt, and who has already said at the Last Supper that his life is "poured out for many" (26.28).

Matthew presents Pilate as a hideous parody of the Messiah. It is the Messiah who comes to set people free, but here it is Pilate who teases the crowd by offering to set free one of their prisoners. It is the Messiah who, though politically committed, is innocent of all wrongdoing, but here it is Pilate who washes his hands, feigning innocence. It is the Messiah who should be attracting the unswerving loyalty of the Jerusalem authorities, but here it is Pilate who has the high priests and scribes at his beck and call. Pontius Pilate is no honest broker but a pale imitation of Jesus.

Luke

Luke mentions Pontius Pilate three times before the passion narrative, and each reference provides a helpful introduction to his role in the story. Pilate first appears tucked in between the emperor Tiberius and the local ruler Herod Antipas in a list of those in control of the region (and whose authority is implicitly questioned by John the Baptist, to whose ministry this list is an introduction) (3.1). He later appears as a governor who executed some Galileans and mixed their blood with their sacrifices (13.1). This portrays him as a ruthless man who doesn't hesitate to break taboos to execute punishment and who apparently fears no reprisal. Then he finally appears in the introduction to the question about paying taxes to Caesar. The scribes and chief priests plot to trap Jesus and hand him over to the governor (22.2). There seems no question that handing Jesus over to the governor means Jesus' fate can be relied upon.

The way Jesus challenges Rome is explicit in Luke's gospel from the very beginning. Gabriel tells Mary that her son will "be great and will be called the Son of the Most High. The Lord God will give him the throne of his father David, and he will reign over the house of Jacob forever; his kingdom will never end" (1.32–33). Mary announces that through her son, the Lord God "has performed mighty deeds with his arm; he has scattered those who are proud in their inmost thoughts. He has brought down rulers from their thrones but has lifted up the humble" (1.51–52). This is hardly encouraging reading for Rome and its allies. Meanwhile Zechariah also realized that God is giving Israel "salvation from our enemies and from the hand of all who hate us" (1.71). The angel tells the shepherds that the baby is Savior and Lord – two titles closely associated with Roman emperors (2.11). And Jesus' reign is to be one of peace – the very state that the *Pax Romana* claimed to bring to all of Rome's subjugated peoples. Jesus' peace is more than the absence of conflict; it is the flourishing of all creation founded on the right worship of God. It is a peace Rome cannot comprehend.

So a showdown between the two global authorities is inevitable. Luke's account has four scenes.

1. The Stirrer and the Unstirred

Then the whole assembly rose and led him off to Pilate. And they began to accuse him, saying, "We have found this man subverting our nation. He opposes payment of taxes to Caesar and claims to be Messiah, a king." So Pilate asked Jesus, "Are you the king of the Jews?" "You have said so," Jesus replied. Then Pilate announced to the chief priests and the crowd, "I find no basis for a charge against this man." But they insisted, "He stirs up the people all over Judea by his teaching. He started in Galilee and has come all the way here." (23.1 – 5)

The contrast in Luke's account is between the Jerusalem authorities and Pilate. The former repeatedly complain that Jesus has been causing trouble throughout Pilate's domain, leading the common people astray. The latter consistently appears to underestimate Jesus.

The Jerusalem authorities show the limits of their imagination (or their tendency to fabrication) by the way they convey Jesus' answers to their questions. On taxes, Jesus places the whole practice of loyalty to Rome within the larger question of loyalty to God (20.25). Likewise on kingship, he places the rule of the status quo within the larger perspective and timescale of the coming of the Son of Man (22.69). If the Jerusalem authorities construe such remarks as a crude thrust for power, Pilate equally misinterprets them as harmless philosophizing. Jesus has none of the trappings of majesty – armed followers, citadels, wealth, a royal entourage – so how can he be a serious threat? Pilate is not stirred and waves his key allies' concerns away without serious consideration.

2. The King and His Parody

On hearing this, Pilate asked if the man was a Galilean. When he learned that Jesus was under Herod's jurisdiction, he sent him to Herod, who was also in Jerusalem at that time. When Herod saw Jesus, he was greatly pleased, because for a long time he had been wanting to see him. From what he had heard about him, he hoped to see him perform a sign of some sort. He plied him with many questions, but Jesus gave him no answer. The chief priests and the teachers of the law were standing there, vehemently accusing him. Then Herod and his soldiers ridiculed and mocked him. Dressing him in an elegant robe, they sent him back to Pilate. That day Herod and Pilate became friends – before this they had been enemies. (23.6 – 12)

Herod is a parody of Jesus. He thinks of himself as a king and has all the royal trappings that Jesus lacks. In an extraordinarily ironic moment, Herod dresses Jesus as a king. Jesus, perhaps overcome by the degree to which Herod has debased the notion of kingship, holy living, and the Jewish people in general, does not even speak to Herod. There is no sign of the kind Herod thought Jesus might be good for.

Herod is also a parody of Pilate. Pilate really does have power – or kingship, or at least an army. He does not seem to be troubled by having disposed of the Galileans (in the way Herod is anxious about having executed John the Baptist [9.7 – 9]). But Herod impresses Pilate by seeming to regard Jesus as beneath his concern. Thus Herod shows himself as impervious to the protests of the Jerusalem authorities. For the first time, Pilate takes Herod seriously; a man who sees Jesus as irrelevant is clearly a man who knows where true power lies.

3. Jesus Is Dismissed as Irrelevant

Pilate called together the chief priests, the rulers and the people, and said to them, "You brought me this man as one who was inciting the people to rebellion. I have examined him in your presence and have found no basis for your charges against him. Neither has Herod, for he sent him back to us; as you can see, he has done nothing to deserve death. Therefore, I will punish him and then release him." (23.13 – 16)

Pilate executes judgement. Neither he nor Herod has genuinely examined Jesus, but it is a mark of his superiority that he considers Jesus unworthy of his attention. To underline Jesus' low status, Pilate resolves to give him a light flogging. (There were three degrees of flogging, and this was less grueling than the others.) Flogging was not so much a punishment as a way of reminding the poor that they were powerless. Torture has been used in a similar way in recent times, not so much to extract information as to humiliate the prisoner and remind everyone who is in absolute control.

4. Pilate's Politics Overcome His Arrogance

With one voice they cried out, "Away with this man! Release Barabbas to us!" (Barabbas had been thrown into prison for an insurrection in the city, and for murder.) Wanting to release Jesus, Pilate appealed to them again. But they kept shouting, "Crucify him! Crucify him!" For the third time he spoke to them: "Why? What crime has this man committed? I have found in him no grounds for the death penalty. Therefore I will have him punished and then release him." But with loud shouts they insistently demanded that he be crucified, and their shouts prevailed. So Pilate decided to grant their demand. He released the man who had been thrown into prison for insurrection and murder, the one they asked for, and surrendered Jesus to their will. (23.18–25)

The crowd's demand is, in the terms of the story so far, totally unreasonable. They ask Pilate to crucify a harmless man of no status and ask for the release of a known revolutionary. Pilate is forced into facing up to his basic political commitments. By not listening to his key allies, the Jerusalem authorities, he has provoked them into making wild demands. His arrogance is getting him into trouble. Much better to remember the alliance that keeps Judea under his and Rome's stranglehold, give the Jerusalem elite their curious request, and avoid jeopardizing the cozy coalition.

Luke's Pilate is no more an honest broker than Matthew's. The difference between the two portrayals is this: in Matthew's version, Pilate knows Jesus is dangerous but is concerned to unload the blame for Jesus' death onto others; in Luke's version, Pilate is never convinced Jesus jeopardizes anything of any significance – what is jeopardized is Pilate's relationship with those who control the common people on his behalf. Pilate's recognition that he needs to shore up this key relationship brings about his change of heart and Jesus' death.

John

John narrates a constant antagonism between Jesus and the people John calls "the Jews". By "the Jews", John refers not to the people of Israel in general (a fact forgotten in centuries of Christian persecution of Jewish people) but to the elite group centered around the high priest and his entourage. Jesus calls himself the "good shepherd" and regards the Jerusalem authorities as "hired hands" or "bandits" (10.1, 8, 11–12). He criticizes their control of the temple as exploitative (2.13–22), and he implies that they are blind to the work of God (9.39–41).

The conflict with "the Jews" is but part of Jesus' deeper conflict with "the world". This is another technical term that means not simply everything that God created but rather refers to everything that rejects the grace of God. Jesus knows the world "hates" him (7.7). Behind the world lies the devil, the "the prince of this world" (12.31). Whenever John uses the term "prince", he is grouping all those who are agents of this "prince of this world"; this includes the Jerusalem authorities (7.26, 48) and Pilate himself.

John's account of Jesus' meeting with Pilate is deftly woven into seven scenes, taking place alternately inside and out. The significance of the location is in each case more than circumstantial, as we shall see.

1. Outside: Jesus Is Handed Over

> Then the Jewish leaders took Jesus from Caiaphas to the palace of the Roman governor. By now it was early morning, and to avoid ceremonial uncleanness they did not enter the palace, because they wanted to be able to eat the Passover. So Pilate came out to them and asked, "What charges are you bringing against this man?" "If he were not a criminal," they replied, "we would not have handed him over to you." Pilate said, "Take him yourselves and judge him by your own law." "But we have no right to execute anyone," they objected. This took place to fulfill what Jesus had said about the kind of death he was going to die. (18.28–32)

The contrast throughout the narrative is between what takes place outside and what takes place inside. Outside, Pilate does what he has to do to maintain his functional but uncomfortable relationship with the Jerusalem authorities; the object of the narrative's criticism is the Jerusalem authorities. Inside, the heart of Pilate's rule is gradually revealed – indeed the heart of the Roman Empire, the justification for all its double-dealing and its velvet fist. And the heart is empty. The fact that John's gospel places Jesus' death on the day of preparation for the Passover emphasizes that Jesus is the Lamb of God. This portrays Pilate as Pharaoh and Rome as Egypt and further condemns the Jerusalem authorities as failed versions of Moses. The additional edge in John's trial scene is provided by the fact that Pilate's soldiers have joined the temple police in arresting Jesus (18.3), hence the authorities' bewilderment that Pilate is now stalling on Jesus' execution.

2. Inside: God's King and the World's King

> Pilate then went back inside the palace, summoned Jesus and asked him, "Are you the king of the Jews?" "Is that your own idea," Jesus asked, "or did others talk to you about me?" "Am I a Jew?" Pilate replied. "Your own people and chief priests handed you over to me. What is it you have done?" Jesus said, "My kingdom is not of this world. If it were, my servants would fight to prevent my arrest by the Jewish leaders. But now my kingdom is from another place." "You are a king, then!" said Pilate. Jesus answered, "You say that I am a king. In fact, the reason I was born and came into the world is to testify to the truth. Everyone on the side of truth listens to me." "What is truth?" retorted Pilate. (18.33–38a)

The first part of this dialogue hangs on John's ambiguous use of the word Jew. On first reading, it seems obvious that Jesus, not Pilate, is a Jew. But in John's gospel, *Jew* means "leader in Jerusalem who has become a quisling of Roman authority". So in this sense, Pilate is more of a Jew than Jesus is. "Your own people" becomes a heavily ironic phrase, since Pilate has the Jerusalem authorities in his pocket.

The "truth" is that God is acting in Jesus to set his people free. Hence it makes sense to talk of Jesus as a king in the sense discussed in relation to the other gospel accounts – a liberator. Pilate cannot see this. He cannot even imagine it. Hence his words, "What is truth?" Inside is empty.

When Jesus says, "My kingdom is not of this world", he is not saying, "I am spiritual and have no interest in the political." He is saying, "I have a kingdom that your imagination – rooted in the 'world', the politics of the devil – cannot comprehend."

3. Outside: Jesus or Barabbas

> With this he went out again to the Jews gathered there and said, "I find no basis for a charge against him. But it is your custom for me to release to you one prisoner at the time of the Passover. Do you want me to release 'the king of the Jews'?" They shouted back, "No, not him! Give us Barabbas!" Now Barabbas had taken part in an uprising. (18.38b – 40)

The true nature of Pilate's alliance with the Jerusalem authorities is revealed in this scene. Pilate regards Jesus' kingdom language as irrelevant because Jesus has said he will not fight (18.36). Meanwhile, the Jerusalem leaders ask for Barabbas – a well-known combatant. In other words, both Pilate and the Jerusalem authorities recognize that violence and military muscle is what counts in the end. Barabbas is safe because he accepts the terms of the battle – a battle everyone knows Pilate will win. What follows is a brutal display of imperial violence.

4. Inside: Romans Flog Jewish Pretensions

> Then Pilate took Jesus and had him flogged. The soldiers twisted together a crown of thorns and put it on his head. They clothed him in a purple robe and went up to him again and again, saying, "Hail, king of the Jews!" And they slapped him in the face. (19.1 – 3)

We are back inside, and there is no veneer of civility any more. The last inside scene revealed the emptiness of Roman rule. This scene reveals its brutality. Pilate shows what Rome does to any-one who claims to be a king. But the scene has plenty of irony. It is gruesome that Pilate is acceding to the wishes of Jesus' own people, who are more protective of Rome than even Pilate is. And Jesus is dressed like Caesar – with a royal purple robe and a crown of thorns (a parody of the emperor's laurel wreath).

5. Outside: Pilate Parades the Prisoner

> Once more Pilate came out and said to the Jews, "Look, I am bringing him out to you to let you know that I find no basis for a charge against him." When Jesus came out wearing the crown of thorns and the purple robe, Pilate said to them, "Here is the man!" As soon as the chief priests and their officials saw him, they shouted, "Cru-cify! Crucify!" But Pilate answered, "You take him and crucify him. As for me, I find no basis for a charge against him." The Jews insisted, "We have a law, and according to that law he must die, because he claimed to be the Son of God." (19.4–7)

Pilate is teasing the Jerusalem authorities by dangling Jesus before them. The scene begins to make sense when one sees Pilate as tormenting them by seeming to toss Jesus to them and then pulling him away. Suggesting they crucify Jesus is a form of hu-miliation – they have no power to do so. The whole scene affirms where power really lies in Jerusalem.

6. Inside: The Power of the World and the Purpose of God

> When Pilate heard this, he was even more afraid, and he went back inside the palace. "Where do you come from?" he asked Jesus, but Jesus gave him no answer. "Do you refuse to speak to me?" Pilate said. "Don't you realize I

have power either to free you or to crucify you?" Jesus answered, "You would have no power over me if it were not given to you from above. Therefore the one who handed me over to you is guilty of a greater sin." From then on, Pilate tried to set Jesus free, but the Jews kept shouting, "If you let this man go, you are no friend of Caesar. Anyone who claims to be a king opposes Caesar." (19.8–12)

Suddenly, the tone of the scene changes. Pilate becomes afraid (I would translate "very" instead of "even more" in 19.8). This man claims to be the Son of God. This is not just a king – a threat to Pilate's own power, although absurd because without violence. This is a god – *the* God – and hence a threat to Caesar himself, and not only to Caesar but to the whole Roman sense of the transcendent. Violence is no longer the issue. This means that Pilate, for the first time, is powerless. He hastens inside and asks the fundamental question, "Where do you come from?"

This is the fundamental question because it is the one that began John's gospel. John begins with a description of where Jesus comes from (1.1–18). A whole host of characters feel their way toward the same discovery – including Nicodemus (3.13), the Samaritan woman (4.25–26), the disciples (6.33), and the people of Jerusalem (7.29). Jesus' response gives the question a twist by turning it on Pilate, saying that Pilate's authority comes "from above" – the same place as Jesus' authority. In these circumstances, the background cries of the Jerusalem authorities sound absurd – painfully absurd. The Jerusalem authorities – who should know all about God – call on Caesar, whom Pilate has just begun to discover is only in power for as long as God's patience lasts. The Jerusalem authorities should know this, so their sin is the greater. The death of Jesus is going to be not the triumph of the Jerusalem authorities or the domination of Rome but the victory of God. One can understand Pilate's panic.

7. Outside: The Betrayal of God and the Handing-Over of Jesus

When Pilate heard this, he brought Jesus out and sat down on the judge's seat at a place known as the Stone Pavement (which in Aramaic is Gabbatha). It was the day of Preparation of the Passover; it was about noon. "Here is your king," Pilate said to the Jews. But they shouted, "Take him away! Take him away! Crucify him!" "Shall I crucify your king?" Pilate asked. "We have no king but Caesar," the chief priests answered. Finally Pilate handed him over to them to be crucified. (19.13–16)

Inside, Pilate has been exposed as empty, powerless, and full of fear. So in his moment of truth, he heads straight outside, thus displaying that he is more dependent on the Jerusalem authorities than anyone could previously have realized – he depends on them to give his authority meaning. All he has left is their subservience. He returns to playing his game with them – the game he plays best, dangling Jesus before them. And finally he elicits the ultimate reversal: "We have no king but Caesar", say the chief priests, a perfect summary of their betrayal as leaders of God's people. Pilate is mesmerized by Jesus; the chief priests are mesmerized by Caesar. Pilate has exposed the emptiness of the chief priests' authority, and Jesus has exposed the emptiness of Pilate's.

WASHING OUR OWN HANDS

We have seen that Matthew (like Mark) portrays Pilate as an expert political manipulator who succeeds in disposing of an apparent threat to his authority while at no stage appearing to shoulder any culpability for doing so. Luke's account suggests that Pilate underestimates Jesus but that he disposes of Jesus in order to maintain his alliance with the Jerusalem authorities. John's is the starkest narrative, in which Jesus is the light of truth that exposes the emptiness of Pilate and the profound betrayal of the temple leadership.

I have followed each account in detail because I believe that together these readings transform our understanding of Jesus' death and the reasons for it. The political option Jesus represented is no remote or abstract ideal; it is a live option today. Its full dimensions will emerge in the course of this book, but at this stage I shall simply highlight two moments in the story of Jesus and Pilate that form a backdrop to what follows.

The first is the moment when Pilate washes his hands (Matt. 27.24). It is a moment that has passed into proverb and cliché and has become part of the vocabulary of self-justification. But it must not be forgotten that it is a charade. Pilate *wants* the crowd to believe that Jesus' death is no responsibility of his. (He has succeeded in persuading untold numbers of Christian readers of the gospel of his "spin" on Jesus' execution.) But he is the governor. He has absolute power. Jesus has come before him, and he disposes of Jesus.

So the first thing the passion narrative teaches about politics is to be very skeptical about anybody who wants to sigh and say, "Really, there's nothing I can do." There is plenty that Pilate can do – but he has established at the beginning that Jesus is a threat, so everything that he does from then on is directed to destroying Jesus. Washing his hands is just a cynical smokescreen.

But what about the more charitable reading? In the more charitable reading, Pilate's hand is forced by the fanaticism of the crowd. In this case, the fault still lies with Pilate. Pilate has no reason to let the crowd force his hand. This is not a democracy (even though the crowd scene falsely suggests it is); he is the governor, and no one in Judea can oust him. The second lesson of this narrative is that those in power do no good by failing to realize the power they have. Power is not wrong or bad or inherently corrupt; it is given for a purpose – to reflect the truth, to set people free – and only becomes sinister when it is not used for the purpose for which it has been given.

Few people today have a monopoly of political power in the way Pilate did. But many people have overwhelming power in smaller spheres – families, churches, voluntary organizations, neighborhoods, businesses, hospital wards, classrooms, building sites, football stands. Such people need to learn from the gospel accounts of Pontius Pilate. It is deeply manipulative to set someone up to be crucified and at the last minute so arrange things that one can deny all responsibility. It is no use allowing others to prevail upon you through persistence, passion, or emotional blackmail if you are in a position where you alone have the power to be just.

And who has such power? The investor has the power to relocate funds to organizations that have a social dividend – for example, those that lend money to disadvantaged people who would normally find it next to impossible to get credit, or those that finance low-cost properties for people struggling to climb onto the housing ladder. The shareholder has the power to oust directors who will not steer their company in the ways of fair and sustainable practices. The voter has the power to unseat a government or local authority that mishandles power. The trustee has the power to intervene in a voluntary organization that is being turned into the poodle of its chief executive. The union member has the power to invoke restraint on oppressive practices or harassment in the workplace. The shopper has the power to purchase fairly traded goods and shun the products of corporations that mistreat their staff or the environment. The football fan has the power to speak to the police about racist chanting in the stands.

On one housing estate there was a large empty field, fenced off by the county council. Local residents had often asked to be able to use it for sport and recreation, but there were always civic reasons why it was not possible – mostly referring to the debris on the park and fears of litigation. One morning two local parents arranged for a street of children to clear the park of cans, bottles, and other litter. They made sure the newspapers were aware. They did not tear down the fences, but they carefully dismantled all the local authority's reasons for keeping the fences up. Soon, soccer matches were being played on the field. The council seemed to be able to find sums of money for equipment after all. It became obvious that attempting to sell the park to a major retail developer would be politically disastrous. Those two parents began with a bottle clear-up. Within weeks they had a youth movement. It turned out they were not as powerless as everyone initially thought.

It is no use saying, "Really, there's nothing I can do." Politics begins when one realizes there is plenty one can do. Discipleship begins when one realizes that what one must do is to do what Jesus did.

"WHAT IS TRUTH?"

John's account of the meeting of Jesus and Pilate shows the emptiness of Pilate's inside, of the inside of his regime in Judea, and ultimately of the inside of the whole Roman Empire. It is summed up in his question, "What is truth?" This is the second key moment in the story of Jesus and Pilate.

Pilate is running a ruthlessly efficient machine. It makes the common people powerless subjects, it makes the social, political, and religious elites willing quislings, and it makes him exception-ally wealthy. Like most ruthless bureaucracies, it doesn't pause too long to ask the question why. The justification for almost every venture is that it will maintain the status quo.

Pilate's world is not as far from today's world as it may at first appear. What they have in common is that truth is a difficult thing to talk about. On a famous occasion, one of Tony Blair's aides intercepted a telling question to the British prime minister with the unforgettable words "We don't do God." In other words, please don't dig down to the truth issues. We're trying to run a bureaucracy that keeps most people happy most of the time. It gets us reelected. Don't unsettle the equilibrium by asking why. The aide was very wise of course – the media uproar whenever a British prime minister refers to ultimate purpose in general or to God in particular (for example when Blair later said that God would be his judge over the Iraq invasion) shows that the British public finds such questions deeply uncomfortable. Pilate would have been quite at home in British political life.

The words "We don't do God" display vividly how public life in Western democracies has settled for an instrumental notion of truth. Something is true if it works, if it gets you to the next place. No one ever discusses what the final place is. For example, in Brit-ain people work very hard so their children can go to the best school. (They either work hard to get a good salary to pay school fees, or they work hard to earn enough money to buy a house in the catchment area of a "good" state school, or they work hard to argue with the education authorities to get their child into such a school.) At the best school, pupils work hard to get to the best uni-versity. Once there, students work hard to get the best results. The best results enable them to get the best jobs. But what are the best jobs? The ones that make enough money to send one's children to the best schools, of course. This is what I mean by an instrumental notion of truth and value. It is a circle from which I cannot escape until I find a different way of defining the word *best*.

For Pilate, all that was to be hoped for was more of the same. Jesus asked him why. He had no answer. Jesus stretched Pilate's imagination farther than it was able to go, and Pilate snapped and went out to resume his merciless taunting of the Jerusalem authorities. Pilate couldn't imagine an order not founded on the threat of violent military force, a competition Rome would always win. But Jesus pointed to an empire not founded on force, an emperor who set his people free, a life not bounded by death – and he called this "the truth". You can see Pilate's brow furrowing, his eyes finding it hard to focus, the solid legs beneath him beginning to shake.

Does Jesus stretch our imaginations? Do we allow him to challenge our instrumental notions of truth? Do we take the risk of letting him dismantle the deftly prepared PowerPoint presentations that tell us how to make our companies, organizations, or families richer, safer, fitter, stronger? Does it suddenly begin to strike us that *we* are Pilate in this story, saying to Jesus, "Don't disturb my carefully ordered world. Don't look at me like that. I'm not powerful. I'm not a manipulator. I'm not a person who finds it best to avoid asking why. I'm not. I'm not. I'm not.... Am I?"

OPPORTUNITIES FOR INDIVIDUAL
OR GROUP REFLECTION

I wonder what are the things in your world that everyone wants.

I wonder who seem to be the most powerful people in your world.

I wonder what it is like to be under the control of someone you could undermine with a single word or gesture if you chose to do so.

I wonder what Pilate did, said, or read before he went to sleep at night.

I wonder what it is like to be tormented by someone who knows he or she has power over you.

I wonder what it feels like to sense truth is against you.

I wonder what it is like to keep every conversation and interaction moving so as to avoid getting on to the question of why.

I wonder what it is like to wash one's hands when one knows one has done a terrible thing.

I wonder what it is like to discover one is more powerful than one had previously realized.

Lord God our Father,
whose Son stood before the governor with his life in
*   the balance:*
we pray for all who stand trial today,
at risk of losing their reputation, their liberty, or their life –
and we recall those who face imprisonment without trial;
we remember before you all who hold public office,
and pray that your Holy Spirit will build them up
not just as experts in procedure and efficiency
but as people who can hear and speak the truth.

Give us grace to discern and evaluate the power we
*   each have,*
through the money we invest, the friends we make, the
*   shares we own,*
the societies we join, the votes we cast, the shops we visit,
the language we use, the letters we write, and the promises
*   we keep:*
have mercy on us for the times we have washed our hands
and said there was nothing we could do;
and renew us as your body, using your power as your
*   Spirit does,*
to set people free for the abundant life you bring
in your Son, Jesus Christ. Amen.

CHAPTER 2

BARABBAS

This chapter is a study in violence. When people feel powerless, and words seem to count for nothing, they are almost bound to feel that they cannot wait any longer and must use what little force they have. Barabbas was probably not a man who had taken a careful, cold look at his chances of success. More likely he was so convinced of the rectitude of his view of the world that he thought anything was justified in pursuit of it. What should we do when we believe we are right but the obstacles in our way are overwhelming?

THE POLITICAL OPTIONS

In the first chapter we looked at the ruthlessness and brutality of Roman rule and the way it successfully harnessed the support of the local elite to underwrite its exercise of power. It seemed there was nothing the people could do. How could the people respond in the face of Roman domination? There were broadly four options.

Collaboration

Collaboration was the only available option for those who aspired to wealth and a degree of power. Rome ruled its empire through the cooperation of local elites. The strategy of the ruling classes is epitomized by Herod the Great, the half-Jewish king who ruled for the generation up to the time of Jesus' birth. Herod reconstructed the Jewish temple on a grand scale, with Roman support and local enthusiasm. Yet on top of the entrance gate to the temple, the focal point of Jewish identity, Herod placed a golden eagle, the symbol of Rome. Herod had brought in a high priestly class, some of whom were not from Judea but were returnees from the spread of the Jewish population around the Mediterranean. Thus the Jewish leaders of Jesus' time represented neither the people nor the empire.

Collaboration involved a sober recognition that the sovereignty of Israel was dead and buried. The restoration of the successors of King David was a fantasy. But collaboration also required confidence that concessions won from Rome were valuable and sustainable. A series of brutal interventions from the Roman governors suggested otherwise; the reality was that the Jerusalem authorities were puppets in the governors' hands.

Reform

The whole ethos of the so-called Deuteronomistic history – the books of the Old Testament such as Samuel and Kings that tell the story of how Israel rose to ascendancy under David and Solomon before collapsing into exile 400 years later – is that exile in Babylon was an inevitable result of the people of God departing from God's ways. Thus the most likely way for literate Jews of Jesus' time to understand their situation under Roman domination was along the same lines – to see it as something the Jews had brought upon themselves. The appropriate response was therefore to reform Jewish ways of life, to return to the holiness to which God called his people.

Perhaps the defining issue in relation to holiness was purity. Jews had a holy land, the land of Israel, and within that land were holy places, arranged in a hierarchy, at the top of which was the Holy of Holies in the Jerusalem temple. They also had holy times, notably the weekly Sabbath, but also festival days such as the Passover, the Day of Atonement, the Feast of Tabernacles, and so on. They had holy persons, again in a hierarchy according to purity, with priests at the top and the physically impaired near the bottom. They had holy bodily marks, notably circumcision. And they had holy things, particularly food, and correspondingly impure things such as dead bodies and bodily fluids.

It was practically and economically impossible for the common people, especially those who worked on the land, to keep these purity codes. The Sadducees were a political and religious party with many wealthy members who accepted only the written law of Moses. They assumed that only the priests could be genuinely holy. This justified the maintenance of an upper class that found common cause with Rome. By contrast, the Pharisees were a political and religious party who defined themselves in opposition to the Sadducees. Their emphasis was more on home than on temple. They sought to enable the masses to observe the purity codes by reinterpreting the codes in applicable ways. The Pharisees' program was a way of concentrating power in their own hands. They, after all, were the only trustworthy arbiters of purity. The program rallied a wide base of popular support for their social power without requiring them to ground that power in genuine identification with the poor. Jesus is constantly seen in conflict with the Pharisees' interpretations of purity and in criticism of their claims to be on the side of the masses.

Withdrawal

For the Essenes the answer to the question of purity lay not in restricting holiness to the few or in extending it to the many; it lay in withdrawal into a rigorous community. Like the option of collusion, withdrawal was a statement that there was little or no possibility of changing the existing order. But like the option of reform, the key issue was seen as restoring holy life in Israel.

The Essene worldview rested on a deep skepticism about the worthiness of the body. Death was to be welcomed because the body was seen as a prison from which the soul was longing to escape. The Essenes sought to purify the mind and stood aloof from temple sacrifices, which they saw as too liable to pollution. Ritual purity was taken very seriously, and the Sabbath was kept to the extent of deferring calls of nature. There was close attention to the sick and generous hospitality to strangers. At least one strand of the movement foresaw an imminent conflict in which God would overcome the forces that oppressed Israel after a gruesome struggle. But there is no evidence that this constituted any kind of vision for violent or nonviolent engagement with the powers that controlled Judea.

Restorationism

The fourth approach might be called violent revolution. But "revolution" is an anachronism. The revolutions of the modern era have invariably been undertaken by those who assumed the old way of doing things was bad and a new way was not only possible but also urgently necessary. In other words, their golden era lay in the future. Such a view was almost inconceivable in Jesus' time. It was universally assumed that the golden era lay in the past and that all that could be desired was a restoration of that previous blessed order. For Jews, that blessed era was generally perceived to be the time of King David, about a thousand years before Christ.

From the reign of Augustus onward, Rome became less concerned with its own perception of the republic's manifest destiny to conquer and rule and more focused on the cult of the emperor himself. Worship of the emperor was intolerable in Jewish Palestine, where the God of Abraham and Moses and David was regarded as the only Lord, so Jewish feasts became significant moments of expressing opposition to Rome.

The Zealots of Jesus' time were as angry with the Jerusalem authorities as they were with Roman rule. Many were peasants from Judea who were exasperated by paying tithes to priests who were often themselves landowners – and who thus benefited from the peasants twice over. Others were lower members of the priestly class. Around them gathered slaves and others who had little to gain from staying within the law. These people were known as bandits. To such people the idea of restoring a long-buried kingly line, of returning to older laws and social customs, and of throwing out the local ruling classes and restoring a previous generation of notables was very appealing.

To get a sense of the kinds of social conditions that fostered the activity of bandits, one need only consider the situation in Iraq after the American-British invasion. Like the Judea of the Gospels, Iraqi society is a traditional agrarian one, and peasants are used to being exploited by landowners and governments. The economic crisis and social disruption of the war produces widespread banditry. The peasant is then torn between, on the one hand, a concern for law and order, and on the other hand, a perception that the bandit shares and often symbolizes: a basic agrarian sense of justice and religious loyalty. It is not always clear whether lawlessness is straightforward criminality or a more fundamental rejection of the status quo.

So the striking feature of the Zealots is not that they were radical and revolutionary, overturning the existing order and ushering in a new era of freedom, equality, and redistributed wealth and power. On the contrary, the Zealots offered little more than

one thing: a change of government, an alteration in the person-
nel operating a system that assumed the domination of the labor-
ing classes by powerful elites. In comparison to Jesus' program,
the Zealots challenged not too much but too little; the problem
was not what they wanted to change but how much they assumed
would stay the same. And the problem with the violent methods
the Zealots used was likewise not that they were too strong but
that they were too weak.

JESUS AND THE ZEALOTS

While Jesus speaks to and about the Sadducees, the Pharisees, and other groups explicitly, the Gospels record no addresses
he makes directly to the Zealots. The reader has to pick up more
subtle gestures and allusions. Some of these draw connections between Jesus and the Zealots. Others distinctly distance Jesus and
his followers from the Zealot movement and its methods.

The most obvious reference to the Zealots comes in the list
of disciples, where one is known as "Simon the Zealot" (Matt.
10.4; Mark 3.18; Luke 6.15; Acts 1.13). Some scholars have speculated that as many as half of the twelve disciples had some kind of
link to the Zealot movement. Some have also suggested that when
Luke mentions "the Galileans whose blood Pilate had mixed with
their sacrifices" (13.1), the true meaning might be "the Galileans
whose blood Pilate had mixed with the blood of their victims",
and the passage might refer to a Zealot uprising, which may con-
cur with other contemporary reports.

Perhaps more fruitful is to recognize that several aspects of
Jesus' message had common features with the Zealot ethos. Jesus
says, "Blessed are you who hunger now, for you will be satisfied.
Blessed are you who weep now, for you will laugh. [But] Woe to
you who are well fed now, for you will go hungry. Woe to you who

laugh now, for you will mourn and weep" (Luke 6.21, 25). This is the kind of thing the Zealots were happy to hear. Likewise, when Jesus set family ties in the larger context of commitment to God's kingdom, the Zealots would have heard a song they would readily sing: "If anyone comes to me and does not hate father and mother, wife and children, brothers and sisters – yes, even life itself – such a person cannot be my disciple" (Luke 14.26). But most of all, the Zealots endorsed Jesus' call for unconditional obedience and the willingness to take discipleship to the point of humiliating, agonizing martyrdom – the cross. "Blessed are those who are persecuted because of righteousness, for theirs is the kingdom of heaven" (Matt. 5.10); "Do not suppose that I have come to bring peace to the earth. I did not come to bring peace, but a sword. For I have come to turn 'a man against his father, a daughter against her mother, a daughter-in-law against her mother-in-law – your enemies will be the members of your own household'" (Matt. 10.34–36). Most of all, there is reasonable ground for inferring that Jesus' clarion call to discipleship derived from a Zealot formula: "Whoever wants to be my disciple must deny themselves and take up their cross and follow me" (Matt. 16.24).

It is also important to recognize that the language Jesus uses about the imminent end of the world also resonates with the Zealot worldview. The Zealots believed that a time was coming when God would deliver his people from Roman oppression and when God alone would rule. Indeed they understood that the time of persecution immediately preceding this deliverance had already begun. They interpreted the famines and the disorganization of Herod's administration as part of this purposeful suffering. The key, as they saw it, was that the people of God acknowledged God as their sole ruler. The Zealots made no distinction between their hopes for the earthly transfer of power from the Romans to themselves and their longings for the heavenly intervention of God as the sole ruler of his people and his world. It was up to humans to cooperate as much as they could with God's coming transformation. While they believed God alone would bring salvation, they were ingenious and skillful in subverting power structures and sacrificial in giving up property and life.

This much shows very significant similarities between Jesus and his followers and the Zealots. But there are equally significant differences. Most importantly, Jesus explicitly renounces violence: "Blessed are the meek, for they will inherit the earth.... Blessed are the peacemakers, for they will be called children of God" (Matt. 5.5, 9); "Love your enemies and pray for those who persecute you, that you may be children of your Father in heaven" (Matt. 5.44–45); " 'Put your sword back in its place,' Jesus said to him, 'for all who draw the sword will die by the sword' " (Matt. 26.52). In addition, he has an inclusive approach to the Gentiles: "Many will come from the east and the west, and will take their places at the feast with Abraham, Isaac and Jacob in the kingdom of heaven" (Matt. 8.11). And he has a very different notion of purity from that of the Zealots: "Go and learn what this means: 'I desire mercy, not sacrifice.' For I have not come to call the righteous, but sinners" (Matt. 9.13). The Zealots could not have comprehended Jesus' parable of the good Samaritan (Luke 10.30–37).

In this context it becomes easier to see the significance of Jesus' words, "The coming of the kingdom of God is not something that can be observed, nor will people say, 'Here it is,' or 'There it is,' because the kingdom of God is in your midst" (Luke 17.20–21), for Jesus was explicitly denying that God had prepared an ordered pattern by which suffering and political revolt would dovetail behind an intervention of God to restore his rule and to vindicate Israel. There was no place for zeal as understood in the Zealot sense as unconditional dedication to violent restoration of godly rule. Instead there was another unconditional command-ment: to love God and neighbor – and even stranger and enemy.

The similarities and differences between Jesus and the Zeal-ots crystallize in two passages from the Gospels. The first is from John's account of the cleansing of the temple. Jesus "made a whip out of cords, and drove all from the temple courts, both sheep and cattle; he scattered the coins of the money changers and over-turned their tables. To those who sold doves he said, 'Get these out of here! Stop turning my Father's house into a market!' His disciples remembered that it is written: 'Zeal for your house will consume me'" (John 2.15–17). Here Jesus appears to act like a Zealot, exhibiting zeal and acting violently. There is no doubt that Jesus shared with the Zealots a desire that Israel refocus its life on God alone. But this was not a violent zeal; the aggression in this account is directed toward sheep, cattle, coins, tables, and doves. No one is hurt, let alone killed. It is a vivid symbolic gesture, not an element of a violent insurrection.

The second passage is Matthew's account of Jesus' arrest. After Judas's kiss, "the men stepped forward, seized Jesus and ar-rested him. With that, one of Jesus' companions reached for his sword, drew it out and struck the servant of the high priest, cut-ting off his ear. 'Put your sword back in its place,' Jesus said to him, 'for all who draw the sword will die by the sword. Do you think I cannot call on my Father, and he will at once put at my disposal more than twelve legions of angels? But how then would the Scriptures be fulfilled that say it must happen in this way?' In that hour Jesus said to the crowd, 'Am I leading a rebellion, that you have come out with swords and clubs to capture me? Every day I sat in the temple courts teaching, and you did not arrest me. But this has all taken place that the writings of the prophets might be fulfilled.' Then all the disciples deserted him and fled" (Matt. 26.50–56). Here Jesus explicitly refers to the Zealots, who were indeed "leading a rebellion". He clearly constitutes a political threat in the eyes of those arresting him, but he makes it clear that his armies are very different from those of the Zealots, and he has no need to use them. But underlying the whole debate is Jesus' intimacy with the Father, something the Zealots' zeal could never realize.

This comparison between Jesus and the Zealots establishes two things. One is that Jesus had established a new form of life that others saw as a political threat. The other is that Jesus had no intention of translating that social program into a violent revolution. The nature of Jesus' new form of life is perhaps best expressed by John Howard Yoder: "There are thus about the new community of disciples those sociological traits most characteristic of those who set about to change society: a visible structured fellowship, a sober decision guaranteeing that the costs of commitment to the fellowship have been consciously accepted, and a clearly defined life-style distinct from that of the crowd.... The distinctness is not a cultic or ritual separation, but rather a nonconformed quality of ('secular') involvement in the life of the world. It thereby constitutes an unavoidable challenge to the powers that be and the beginning of a new set of social alternatives."[1]

JESUS AND BARABBAS

All the gospel writers portray the crowd choosing Barabbas over Jesus. In chapter 1, we saw that the Jerusalem authorities represented the first political option outlined above. Here we are assuming that Barabbas represents the fourth political option. Whether he was formally a Zealot, the gospel writers do not choose to tell us. The point is that Jesus' way and Barabbas's way are presented in stark contrast – and the crowd chooses Barabbas. Let us now look at the four gospel treatments of this choice.

Matthew

Now it was the governor's custom at the Festival to release a prisoner chosen by the crowd. At that time they had a well-known prisoner whose name was Jesus Barabbas. So when the crowd had gathered, Pilate asked them, "Which one do you want me to release to you: Jesus Barabbas, or Jesus who is called the Messiah?" For he knew it was out of envy that they had handed Jesus over to him. While Pilate was sitting on the judge's seat, his wife sent him this message: "Don't have anything to do with that innocent man, for I have suffered a great deal today in a dream because of him." But the chief priests and the elders persuaded the crowd to ask for Barabbas and to have Jesus executed. "Which of the two do you want me to release to you?" asked the governor. "Barabbas," they answered. "What shall I do, then, with Jesus who is called the Messiah?" Pilate asked. They all answered, "Crucify him!" "Why? What crime has he committed?" asked Pilate. But they shouted all the louder, "Crucify him!" When Pilate saw that he was getting nowhere, but that instead an uproar was starting, he took water and washed his hands in front of the crowd. "I am innocent of this man's blood," he said. "It is your responsibility!" All the people answered, "His blood is on us and on our children!" Then he released Barabbas to them. But he had Jesus flogged, and handed him over to be crucified. (27.15–26)

"Abba" means "father" in an intimate sense, as often used by Jesus, notably in the Lord's Prayer (6.9). The prefix "Bar" means "son" – as in Barnabas, Bartimaueus, Bartholemew, and Simon Bar-Jonah. In Arabic the prefix would be "Abu", as in the notorious Palestinian leader Abu Nidal and the military prison west of

Baghdad known as Abu Ghraib. In Scotland the prefix would be Mac or Mc as in Macdonald, while in Ireland it would be O' as in O'Kane.

Thus the crowd has a choice between "Jesus, son of the father" (Barabbas) and Jesus Christ, also son of the Father. The parallel between the two could not be clearer. Matthew repeatedly sets the two alongside each other: "Which one?" (27:17), "Jesus Barabbas, or Jesus who is called the Messiah?" (v. 17), "Which of the two?" (v. 21), "'Barabbas' ... 'What shall I do, then, with Jesus?'" (v. 21–22), "he released Barabbas ... But he had Jesus flogged" (v. 26).

And not only is this choice a stark one; it is also one with a large audience. Like the last scene of a play, it seems as though every character has found their way back onto the stage. We have the Roman governor, the colluding Jewish authorities, the restorationist Zealot, and the wavering crowd. The only ones missing are the disciples. Significantly, the scene is played out on Roman territory and according to Roman rules; like at the end of a gladiator contest, which generally took place between bandits – condemned criminals or those who had fought against Rome – the crowd would choose which combatant would die and which would live.

So for Matthew, the issue is profoundly one of choice. The crowd has a choice between two people called Jesus, one who seeks peace, the other who practices violence. The reader has a choice between alternative readings of the nature of Jesus' threat to Rome, a threat explored in the previous chapter. And the church has a perpetual choice of which Jesus to follow. And, uncompromisingly, Matthew hammers home the responsibility of that choice: the crowd accepts it, Pilate tries pitifully to evade it, but there is no doubt by the end of this scene that the choice offered at this moment in history is the definitive choice that exposes the truth about each one of us.

Mark

Now it was the custom at the Festival to release a prisoner whom the people requested. A man called Barabbas was in prison with the insurrectionists who had committed murder in the uprising. The crowd came up and asked Pilate to do for them what he usually did. "Do you want me to release to you the king of the Jews?" asked Pilate, knowing it was out of envy that the chief priests had handed Jesus over to him. But the chief priests stirred up the crowd to have Pilate release Barabbas instead. "What shall I do, then, with the one you call the king of the Jews?" Pilate asked them. "Crucify him!" they shouted. "Why? What crime has he committed?" asked Pilate. But they shouted all the louder, "Crucify him!" Wanting to satisfy the crowd, Pilate released Barabbas to them. He had Jesus flogged, and handed him over to be crucified. (15.6–15)

In Mark's account the chief priests are so certain that their true enemy is Jesus that they build an extraordinary coalition of support against him. Not only do they enlist the crowd (whose inability to be holy by the priestly criteria we noted earlier); they also stand alongside the Roman governor, a figure who keeps them in subservience; and to complete their alliance, they call on Barabbas, a murderer and a revolutionary, a man who was looking for their own assassination and the removal of their whole class from power. This is quite an extraordinary selection of allies.

Mark is much more explicit than Matthew in saying that the crowd's choice is between two kinds of revolutionary. On the one hand there is Barabbas. Barabbas's form of revolution is to assassinate key political figures. They must die so that the people may be free, although whether the people genuinely become free by this method is rather doubtful. Not only is the approach doomed to failure and likely to invite a backlash from the might of Rome; more subtly, it is not clear that Barabbas promises to do anything other than change the government. The system is very unlikely to change.

By contrast, on the other hand, is Jesus – the real revolutionary. Jesus does not assume that others must die so that he may be free. He recognizes that he must die so that others may be free. Freedom is not worth killing for, but it is worth dying for. Jesus does exactly what he expects his followers to do: he denies himself and takes up his cross. Jesus is a real revolutionary because he promises a totally new empire – not the rule of Caesar but the kingdom of God; a completely new form of rule – not being served but serving; a vastly different manner of ushering in the new regime – not the horse of war but the donkey of peace; and a unique mode of transformation – not revolution but resurrection.

Luke

> With one voice they cried out, "Away with this man! Release Barabbas to us!" (Barabbas had been thrown into prison for an insurrection in the city, and for murder.) Wanting to release Jesus, Pilate appealed to them again. But they kept shouting, "Crucify him! Crucify him!" For the third time he spoke to them: "Why? What crime has this man committed? I have found in him no grounds for the death penalty. Therefore I will have him punished and then release him." But with loud shouts they insistently demanded that he be crucified, and their shouts prevailed. So Pilate decided to grant their demand. He released the man who had been thrown into prison for insurrection and murder, the one they asked for, and surrendered Jesus to their will. (23.18 – 25)

Luke's account of the encounter between Jesus and Barabbas has less emphasis on the contrast between the two as revolutionary figures. It is important to remember that in Luke's account, as we explored earlier, Pilate consistently underestimates Jesus. Thus this scene is a little like a pantomime, in which the crowd (and the reader) can see something that the central character, Pilate, cannot see. It is as if Pilate is a tottering Baron Hardup, and the crowd, like the audience at a pantomime, keeps shouting, "He's behind you", as Pilate keeps failing to notice the danger Jesus poses.

Many Christians over the centuries, both the humble believer and the exalted leader, have been eager to maintain that Jesus was innocent. This is understandable, because from the beginning Christians have believed that Christ was tempted as we are yet was without sin (Heb. 4.15). But the scene between Jesus, Pilate, and Barabbas makes little or no sense if one does not appreciate that Jesus posed a genuine threat to the Roman governor. The fact that Jesus was without sin made that threat even greater. If the question was "Has Jesus said and done things that challenge Roman rule in Judea?" the answer was undoubtedly "Yes". This is why it was inevitable that Jesus would die a violent death.

But people still cling on to the idea that Jesus was not just sinless but innocent – that is, no threat to Rome. There are broadly three assumptions those who insist on Jesus' innocence make. One focuses entirely on salvation, understood in a narrowly personal rather than a social sense. On this view, Jesus came primarily to die as a sacrificial lamb to atone for the sins of the world. The precise historical circumstances of Jesus' death are not of great significance to this reading, although the fact that Jesus was rejected by his own people only exacerbates the sin for which Jesus' death was a necessary expiation.

A second assumption is that Jesus was a spiritual figure whose interest was not in the reordering of society but in the reorientation of the soul. From this perspective Jesus' approach to the political crisis in Jerusalem at the time of his death would be always to point to its limited, ephemeral character and to highlight the infinite, lasting character of God. Again the details of Jesus' death are not especially important to this reading, except that they display the full horror of sin (in the face of Judas and the high priests) and the true quality of forgiveness (in Jesus' merciful words from the cross).

The third assumption is that Jesus was a simple agrarian figure, telling whimsical stories with poignant twists, drawing a band of followers from rural peasants and fishermen, and generally having the knockabout fun of a troupe of medieval players. This view tends to see Jesus' death as a pointless tragedy – a terrible misunderstanding of the motives and methods of a harmless troubadour. The moral of the crucifixion story seems largely to be that the world is a cruel and dangerous place, and childlike simplicity is always going to be trodden down.

Widespread as these assumptions are, they ignore the shape and detail of Luke's gospel. Jesus announces the coming reign of God (4.18–21), invites participants (5.8–11), demonstrates its transforming character (5.12–13), makes explicit its demands and rewards (6.17–36), and describes its unique gift (15.11–31). This is not a simple uneducated figure, or a prophet uninterested in human society, or a person whose life is subsumed in his inevitable death. Jesus is bringing a transformation for which the word *revolution* is an inadequate but suitably alarming understatement. Pilate, the Jerusalem authorities, Barabbas, and the crowd are all unable to grasp the true significance of the transformation brought by Jesus. Like pantomime characters, they look foolish from the audience's perspective. But unlike pantomime characters, they can do untold damage.

John

> With this he went out again to the Jews gathered there and said, "I find no basis for a charge against him. But it is your custom for me to release to you one prisoner at the time of the Passover. Do you want me to release 'the king of the Jews'?" They shouted back, "No, not him! Give us Barabbas!" Now Barabbas had taken part in an uprising. (18.38b – 40)

John's account is the least detailed, and it gives no indication that Pilate stood Jesus and Barabbas up as alternatives in a gladiatorial contest, in the way that Matthew portrays and the other two gospel accounts imply. But John's brief account includes two key terms that complete our picture of the contrast between Jesus and Barabbas.

The first term is "Passover". Matthew and Mark refer to the custom of releasing one prisoner at the "Festival", but only John highlights at this point in the story that we are talking about the Passover. This reference identifies that this scene between Pilate, Jesus, Barabbas, and the crowd is a microcosm of the gospel story as a whole. Pilate is like Pharaoh in the story of the exodus. He holds Jesus in chains just as Pharaoh held the Hebrews in slavery. Jesus is the Passover Lamb whose blood anointed the doorposts of the Israelites and delivered them from the death-dealing angel of the Lord. Barabbas is the unworthy people of God, given the offer of life by the self-giving love of God in Jesus. Barabbas's sin was in the past, and a new possibility of life under God was available to him from that moment. The crowd represents the fragility and fickleness of God's people. Even after they have been given the new possibility of life by Jesus, they still choose death in Barabbas. Here is the drama, the tragedy, the grace, and the opportunity of the gospel all in a single moment.

The second term is "bandit" – the single word that is here translated, appropriately, "had taken part in an uprising". John has used the term bandit before. Twice he directly contrasts Jesus' ministry with that of the bandits – translated "robbers": "anyone who does not enter the sheep pen by the gate, but climbs in by some other way, is a thief and a robber. The one who enters by the gate is the shepherd of the sheep" (10.1 – 2). "All who have come before me are thieves and robbers, but the sheep have not listened to them. I am the gate; whoever enters through me will be saved. They will come in and go out, and find pasture. The thief comes only to steal and kill and destroy; I have come that they may have life, and have it to the full" (10.8 – 10). In these contexts, it seems clear that the bandits are the very people who are supposedly leading Israel – the Jerusalem authorities who were so intent on having Jesus crucified. Yet taken together, John 10 and John 18 seem to be saying that the Jerusalem leadership and Barabbas are equally estranged from Jesus. Jesus is the true shepherd, the genuine leader of the people; the thieves and bandits, collaborators and Zealots, are as bad as each other in betraying God's call to be a holy nation.

STRIVING FOR PURITY

I have claimed that Jesus was a real revolutionary in a way that Barabbas and the Zealots were not. I want now to explain that claim under three headings, the first of which is purity. As I have demonstrated, purity lay at the heart of Jewish objection to Roman rule and at the heart of the way different parties responded to it. The high priests were content as long as their own purity and that of their sacrifices were not compromised. The Pharisees saw the land as polluted by Roman occupation and sought to develop an inner purity. The Essenes believed purity was possible only in a secluded community. The Zealots believed no purity really counted as long as the Romans were still present.

Jesus constantly overturns such notions of purity. When the Pharisees see his disciples eating food without ritually washing their hands, Jesus says, "Nothing outside you can defile you by going into you. Rather, it is what comes out of you that defiles you" (Mark 7.15). When Simon the Pharisee criticizes Jesus for letting a notorious woman wash his feet, Jesus says to the woman, "Your sins are forgiven" (Luke 7.48). And perhaps definitively, when Jesus goes to the cross, he knows the Scripture that reads, "Anyone who is hung on a pole is under God's curse" (Deut. 21.23). And yet the cross becomes the hinge of renewed fellowship with God.

The transformation in purity Jesus brings is most vividly displayed in his encounter with the woman who had been bleeding for twelve years (Mark 5.25–34). The woman, whose sickness made her permanently unclean, came up behind Jesus and touched the ritual fringes on the hem of his cloak. Immediately she was healed. The significance of this story is the way it shows that, for Jesus, infection works contrary to the expectations of Pharisees or Zealots. It is not that the woman's disease makes Jesus unclean; on the contrary, it is Jesus' holiness that cleanses the woman. Jesus' holiness is highly infectious – the woman only touches the hem of his cloak and she is transformed. No longer is life lived in perpetual anxiety about becoming defiled; with Jesus, life is lived in perpetual anticipation of being transformed.

This contrast is epitomized on the cross, when the two "bandits" hang either side of Jesus. The first takes into his body the defilement of his punishment and tempts Jesus just as Jesus had been tempted at the beginning of his ministry: "Save yourself and us!" (Luke 23.39). But the other is transformed by the holiness of Jesus, and Jesus' promise of salvation transcends the agony of the scene.

We could imagine that contemporary culture has left such notions of purity behind. But it is not so. All the ways the Pharisees and the Zealots worried about purity are still with us. They were obsessed about food. Today's consumers are similarly obsessed about food. Once we assume "you are what you eat", we open the door to endless anxiety about dietary supplements, food allergies, the language of contamination, and hysteria over food scares. Once we have ceased to focus on the resurrection of the body, we quickly become concerned with seeking perfection in our current body. How we eat becomes linked to a whole pattern that stretches from the gym to the beauty salon. The underlying danger is the same as that of the Zealots: thinking we can become pure by our own efforts.

And it is not just food. The question of race and nationality is profoundly one of purity. Those who object to the immigration of people fleeing persecution or looking for better economic opportunities are very often quickly talking about "polluting" some kind of national blood or character. The Zealots were no different. But Jesus' idea of purity had no time for any notion of the purity of race. The direction implied in the word *pollution* is the opposite of the kingdom's trajectory. God's people are not in danger of being polluted. Instead, it is they who are infectious, always about to be agents of transformation.

And to bring matters into the home and classroom, what parent of dependent children is not anxious that his or her offspring may fall in with the wrong crowd of friends? Do parents who have sought to bring their children up in the Christian faith really believe every day that it is not what goes into a person that defiles him or her but what comes out? The desire for purity is found nowhere more than in the quest for the perfect child, in a cosseted environment with hand-picked friends and a carefully balanced diet.

And purity is also, almost inevitably, about sex. One young person who was beginning to sense he had met the person he was going to marry reflected ruefully on the shortcomings of previous relationships: the fumblings in the dark, the lies to parents, the late nights and bleary-eyed mornings at college, the wondering who realized (and who cared), and the humiliatingly pragmatic conversations about preventing consequences. He spoke to a wise friend, who simply said, "Did it make you happy?" "No", said the young man, without hesitation. "Well", said the friend, "I see it then as a matter for compassion rather than condemnation. Don't forget that Christianity is not so much about being clean as about being cleansed. Don't be so tough on yourself that you cannot see the glory of forgiveness and the gift God is giving you in this new relationship. The purity that matters most is your unambiguous willingness to accept the new life God is giving you in Jesus."

So to say Jesus brought a revolution whereas the Zealots did not is to refer to the way Jesus transformed the notion of purity. Holiness is not an achievement secured by keeping oneself unsullied by the world. It is an infectious disease caught by keeping close to Jesus and to the people with whom he spent his time.

THREE KINDS OF SACRIFICE

Sacrifice is the word at the heart of Zealot appeal, then and now. It is the word that makes war seem meaningful, the word that structures the logic of corporate violence. What does the story of Jesus and Barabbas have to say to a soldier today, one who is sent to be a sacrifice to the causes his or her country believes to be good? And how does one commemorate those who have died in a war that one may not personally have believed was just? Three kinds of sacrifice come to mind in relation to the pursuit of change – or justice – through war.

The first is the sacrifice of the unwillingness to kill. When we send soldiers to war, we ask them to overturn everything we teach them about life. Barabbas lived in a world where violence and oppression were daily realities. This is not true for most Western soldiers commissioned today. Consider this story of a soldier in the Second World War. The soldier was among a company being attacked by a sniper. The sniper was in a fishing shack and was picking off soldiers one by one. The soldier was terrified by fear, but he broke into the shack and found himself in an empty room. There was a door to another room. He realized he needed to break this second door down, but he feared that when he did so the sniper would kill him. But when the soldier broke the door down, he discovered that the sniper was stuck in a sniper harness and could not turn around fast enough. The soldier recalled, "He was entangled in the harness, so I shot him with a revolver, and I felt remorse and shame. I can remember whispering foolishly, 'I'm sorry' and then just throwing up ... I threw up all over myself. It was a betrayal of what I'd been taught since a child." Suddenly this man was isolated. He discovered he was a killer. Unlike Barabbas, this was not what he thought faithfulness inherently entailed.

Here is another account, this time of a friend listening as a Vietnam War veteran talked one afternoon in a parish hall. Beside the bar, an older woman began to attack him. "You got no right to snivel about your little half-baked war. World War Two was a real war. Were you even alive then? *Huh?* I lost a brother in World War Two." The two friends tried to ignore her; she was only a local character. But finally the veteran had had enough. He looked at her and calmly, coldly said, "Have you ever had to kill anyone?" "Well, no!" she answered belligerently. "Then what right have *you* got to tell *me* anything?" There was a long, painful silence throughout the hall, as would occur in a home where a guest had just witnessed an embarrassing family argument. Then the friend asked quietly, "When you got pushed just now, you came back with the fact that you had to kill in Vietnam. Was that the worst of it for you?" "Yeah," he said. "That's half of it." The friend waited for a very long time, but the veteran didn't go on. He only stared into his beer. Finally the friend had to ask, "What was the other half?" "The other half was that when we got home, nobody understood."

And this is the second sacrifice we expect of our soldiers. We expect them to enter a level of experience that separates them from community, to enter a world of silence, because nobody who has not had to make that sacrifice really understands. Comrades in arms have a level of intimacy that is enhanced by the sense of suffering for the pursuit of a higher good. Soldiers often form bonds with one another that are stronger than the bonds they have with their wives. And remembering the sacrifice of soldiers recognizes the dignity of this intimacy and its cost. For it is not just the fallen we remember; it is those whose lives were never the same again – soldiers, families, and friends. We hear the echo of the veteran's words, "Nobody understood." Remembering is a small gesture to say, "At least we are trying." Our silence is a silence of gratitude and an effort to understand.

But there is a third sacrifice that derives directly from the contrast of Barabbas and Jesus. And that is the sacrifice of the cross. Jesus went to the cross as one who knew that his embodiment of God's never-ending love meant he was going to have to face death. But the shape of the Old and New Testaments presents Jesus' sacrifice as making sense only as the *last* sacrifice, the one that finally took away sin and inaugurated the peaceful flourishing of all creation in God's company. The sacrifice of the Son of God is the sacrifice to end all sacrifices. So the war to end all wars was not the First World War; it was the cross. The good news of the cross is fundamentally that the war is over. When we gather at the altar, when we recall the cross by breaking the bread of Christ's body, when we share the banquet of Christ's resurrection in bread and wine, we celebrate the good news that the war, the real war – against sin, death, and the devil – is over.

And that is a truth to die for. But not necessarily a truth to kill for. That is the difference between Jesus and Barabbas. For how can we share that good news with someone we have killed? And yet, ninety years on from the war to end all wars, 2,000 years on from the resurrection that proclaimed the war over, we are still asking our soldiers to make these awesome sacrifices. And with astonishing courage and dignity, they continue to do so. Sometimes I think if we asked our heavenly Father what the worst part of the cross was, he would pause for a long time and say, "the sacrifice of my only Son ... that was half of it." And if we waited in a terrible silence and finally found courage to ask, "What was the other half?" he would say, "The other half was that 2,000 years later, nobody understands."

CHANGING TOO LITTLE

The choice between Barabbas and Jesus, a choice that I am suggesting is a central choice in the whole gospel story, is not a choice between a man who took a political route and a man who took a spiritual route. It is not a choice between a man who wanted outer change and a man who called people to inner change. It is a choice between a man who changed too little and a man who changed everything.

Barabbas changed too little. Yes, he had weapons. Yes, he had plans – to unsettle the cozy alliance between the Romans and the Jerusalem authorities. Yes, he had supporters. Yes, in his wake people lay dead, tensions grew, national resurgence seemed a possibility. But fundamentally Barabbas and the Zealots still believed that what mattered was who the government was. They still believed that armies steered the tiller of history. They were still in thrall to what they took to be the forces that shape reality.

And those forces were exactly what Jesus changed. Jesus did not come to underwrite the forces that everyone understood to shape reality. He came to change them. Yet even today people assume that Barabbas was right: that government is the veil civilized societies put over the fist of naked power, that hidden forces such as markets and economics use their unseen hand to determine the course of history, and that Jesus was a bobbing buoy for truth and virtue who was swept out to sea by the surge of these irresistible waves. But to believe in Jesus is to perceive how profound was the change that Jesus brought. After Jesus, history swung on a new axis. The center of the universe became cross and resurrection.

The cross was for Jesus something it could never be for Barabbas. For Barabbas, the cross meant the rubbing out of opposition, the confrontation with the ruthlessness of Rome, and the personal cost of what he must have hoped would be a national triumph. For Jesus, the cross was the place where God took into and upon himself the whole ghastly horror of human sin and folly. In the resurrection of Jesus, God turned this horror into glory. Just as Jesus took the woman's twelve years of bleeding into himself and emitted healing and salvation, so through cross and resurrection God took sin and death into himself and emitted joy. Jesus wasn't changing just the government; he was changing the very heart of reality.

This is the transformation of reality. This is a change Barabbas could not even imagine, let alone bring about. Barabbas represented an endless sequence of violence. He was a man of some desire to set Israel free and some desire to make something for himself, a man whose story offered yet another element in an endless catalogue of injustice, resentment, recklessness, and punishment. Jesus represented a fundamental transformation of the forces that seemed to make lives like Barabbas' inevitable, an inbreaking of the kingdom of heaven, a shower of grace. The crowd chose Barabbas. And, most of the time, they still do.

OPPORTUNITIES FOR INDIVIDUAL
OR GROUP REFLECTION

I wonder what it is like to feel you have to cooperate even when you must lose something precious to do so.

I wonder what it is like to be told you are impure.

I wonder what it is like always to have a sense of a golden era in the past when everything was just right.

I wonder what it is like to know two very different people who have the same name.

I wonder what it is like to look back and realize everything depended on one choice.

I wonder what makes people find reasons why Jesus is irrelevant to our political life today.

I wonder what your purity code is.

I wonder what it is like to be asked to make a sacrifice that really matters.

I wonder what real changes in history people like Barabbas have ever brought about.

Lord God of transforming grace,
whose Son Jesus stood beside Barabbas
in a grotesque game of "Freedom Idol":
we pray for all who live under tyranny,
national, cultural, or domestic;
we recall all who pursue paths of collaboration,
renewal, withdrawal, or violent resistance;
especially we remember those who serve in the armed forces,
and know the cost of risking their lives
for the ideologies and pride of others.

Help us to recognize before you the ways
our lives deny your Son's transformation:
our obsession with forms of purity
that do not reflect your compassion and forgiveness;
our offering of and demand for sacrifices
that do not bring reconciliation or make us holy;
and our resort to hasty and violent solutions
to profound and common problems.

Make us a people who learn how to choose well,
and seek your society amongst outcasts,
your rule amongst servants,
and your power in the resurrection of your Son;
so that when we stand in the crowd on the day of reckoning
we may sing the song not of Barabbas
but of your Son, Jesus Christ. Amen.

CHAPTER 3

JOSEPH OF ARIMATHEA

The question in this chapter is whether it is possible to be a Christian privately. Many people, not just non-Christians, assume Christian faith is fundamentally a private matter. But the death and resurrection of Jesus changed the heart of reality – and that can hardly be a private thing. Is it possible to hold a Christian faith and leave the outward circumstances of one's life unaltered?

CRYPTO-CHRISTIANS AMONG THE RULING CLASSES

It is easy to see that Jesus stirred the imagination of many people in the Israel of his time. Some dropped everything and followed him. But others, no doubt, had a lot to lose. They had connections. They had wealth. They had influence. They would lose all three if it became known that they were following the man from Nazareth.

As we have seen, the Gospels take a dim view of the Jewish aristocracy of the time. Each dimension of the ruling class is portrayed as deeply damaging to the calling of Israel. In the first place there are the Herodians, gathered around Herod the Great and his sons. Matthew identifies Herod the Great in vivid terms as a rein-carnation of Pharaoh, killing the sons of Israel just as Pharaoh did in the time of Moses (Matt. 2.16–18; Ex. 1.16). Matthew and Mark both show the inner corruption of Herod Antipas's rule when they tell of the execution of John the Baptist. Further, marriages were made with no regard to Jewish law, young women entertained the leading men of the regime in scenes of drunken debauchery, and crucial decisions of life and death were made in a reckless manner with no concern for justice (Matt. 14.1–12; Mark 6.14–29).

Next there are the scribes, for whom Mark reserves his special hostility. They were drawn from both the landed aristocracy and the priestly class, and they built up a considerable power base through their domination of key roles in education, justice, and government. They were widely chosen to lead synagogues, become community elders, and serve as judges. They represented the legal and political status quo, and, inevitably, Jesus frequently came into conflict with them. (The Sermon on the Mount ends with the crowd's astonishment that Jesus taught "as one who had authority, and not as their teachers of the law" [Matt. 7.29].) And this was beside the question of their abuse of privilege for their own social and economic advancement. Even the scribe who engages with Jesus in discussion over which commandment is the greatest – a conversation that ends in agreement about loving God and neighbor – is described as no more than "not far from the kingdom of God" (Mark 12.34). It seems this is the closest a scribe can get.

In the previous chapter we observed the shortcomings of the Sadducees. But it may be helpful to introduce this chapter with a further succinct description of the strengths and weaknesses of the Pharisees, particularly as seen by John. The Pharisees were seen as the more "progressive" party in first-century Judaism because they accepted the oral law – including the relatively recent belief in the resurrection of the dead. Whereas for most parties it was a straight choice between calculating collaboration with Rome and violent resistance, the Pharisees had the moral resources for nonviolent resistance because they believed God would vindicate them in the hereafter even if he did not immediately intervene in the present. After the temple was destroyed during the rebellion of AD 66–70, the Pharisees successfully transferred the center of Jewish faith from temple to home, from sacrifice to community meal. This for the first time meant women could play a full role in ceremonial life. The Pharisees were also highly successful in forming a religion of regular purity, study of the Law, and common meals that sat easily within the broadly Greek culture of the eastern Mediterranean.

Where the Pharisees and the early Christians really parted company was in the latter's understanding of Jesus as the Messiah. Over and over again the early Christians found passages in the Hebrew Scriptures that they saw as unambiguously pointing to the coming of the Messiah in just the way Jesus had become incarnate (e.g., Isaiah 9, Isaiah 53, Micah 5). But the Pharisees said these passages had never been understood as messianic before. The heart of Pharisaism was claiming the authority to interpret the Word of God. The early Christians challenged this authority with their new doctrine of Jesus the Messiah, and so they increasingly came to be thrown out of the synagogues. Wes Howard-Brook explains the Christians' challenge perfectly:

> To be a member of the Chosen People for them was no longer a matter of ethnicity or inheritance but of commitment to belief in Jesus the messiah and the public and personal consequences of that belief.
>
> Ultimately, this self-understanding led to the reversal of the Pharisees' challenge. If the Johannine community

[the community of people in which John's gospel was written] would be expelled from the synagogue if it proclaimed Jesus' messiahship, then those Pharisees who did believe in Jesus must *renounce their status as Pharisees* (John 3.1–11, 9.40–41, 12.42–43, 19.38–42). What came to be the most bitter battle between the Johannine community and mainstream Judaism was against those among the Pharisees who, while recognizing Jesus' authority from God, attempted to be believers from within the Jewish establishment. For the Johannine community, "crypto-Christians" were the hardest to accept. The more Jesus' disciples over the first generations experienced the pain of rejection by their fellow Jews, the more difficult it was to deal with "secret" believers who would not put their lives where their hearts were.[2]

Can one be a Christian on the quiet? Can one be a ruler by day and a worshiper by night? The story of Jesus' passion presents two figures who sought to do just that: Joseph of Arimathea and Nicodemus. It is time to look at how the gospel writers portray these two nocturnal disciples.

JOSEPH OF ARIMATHEA

Each gospel describes Jesus' crucifixion and the moment of his death. Matthew, Mark, and Luke all conclude their account of Jesus' death with a note that his female followers were faithful to the last. John concludes by observing that the circumstances of Jesus' death closely follow the expectations of the Hebrew Scriptures. Then each at this same moment introduces a new character, Joseph of Arimathea, who steps forward to take away the body of Jesus. But the gospel writers vary in their estimation of this character.

Matthew

> As evening approached, there came a rich man from Arimathea, named Joseph, who had himself become a disciple of Jesus. Going to Pilate, he asked for Jesus' body, and Pilate ordered that it be given to him. Joseph took the body, wrapped it in a clean linen cloth, and placed it in his own new tomb that he had cut out of the rock. He rolled a big stone in front of the entrance to the tomb and went away. (27.57–60)

Matthew tells us a great deal in four short verses. Joseph is a rich man. Matthew has earlier recorded Jesus' words that "it is easier for a camel to go through the eye of a needle than for the rich to enter the kingdom of God" (Matt. 19.24). So Joseph is an unlikely disciple. We have seen some of the ways in which people became rich under the Romans, and few of them were honorable. But rather than use his wealth as a wall to insulate himself from danger, Joseph uses it as an opportunity for sacrificial discipleship. He takes the risk of going to see the governor and asking for Jesus' body. He becomes the disciple who takes the place of Peter, James, and the rest. John the Baptist's disciples were on hand to take his body away, but Jesus' body requires a new figure, emerging from the shadows. In burying Jesus, Joseph does what the rich young man in Matthew 19.22 fails to do: he puts his life at risk and gives to the poor.

Joseph takes his place alongside two other distinguished Josephs in the Bible as a man of honor. Joseph of Nazareth does the decent thing at Jesus' conception and birth; Joseph of Arimathea does the decent thing at Jesus' death. Both recall Joseph of Egypt, way back in the Genesis story, a figure whose setbacks became the opportunities for God's outworking of providence, and a man who discovered that God's purposes are never thwarted, however unpromising the circumstances. Like Joseph of Egypt, Joseph of Arimathea is not intimidated by the power of the mighty.

Here Joseph of Arimathea does six things. He takes, wraps, places, cuts, rolls, and goes away. This is a lesson in simple discipleship. We are told nothing of Joseph's motives or inner feelings, be they guilt or sorrow. All we know is that he is a disciple, he is rich, he finds the courage to go to Pilate, and he does these six things. Because the sequence starts with the word "took", one cannot help but recall the four actions of Jesus' last meal with the disciples – took, blessed, broke, and gave (Matt. 26.26). If Jesus demonstrated the simplicity of what he wanted from his disciples, Joseph is the first disciple to obey.

Luke

> Now there was a man named Joseph, a member of the Council, a good and upright man, who had not consented to their decision and action. He came from the Judean town of Arimathea, and he himself was waiting for the kingdom of God. Going to Pilate, he asked for Jesus' body. Then he took it down, wrapped it in linen cloth and placed it in a tomb cut in the rock, one in which no one had yet been laid. It was Preparation Day, and the Sabbath was about to begin. (23.50–54)

Luke's account acknowledges that Joseph is a member of the Sanhedrin, the council that condemned Jesus and sent him to Pilate for execution. But Luke is anxious to portray Joseph in the best possible light. He was a good man and an upright one – a keeper of the Law. He was waiting for the kingdom of God – in other words, while the Pharisees and Sadducees in contrasting ways conformed to or at least accommodated the political status quo, Joseph (like Simeon in the temple at the beginning of Luke's story) was longing for God to come to restore his relationship with Israel, transforming the earthly and heavenly state of affairs. He has the courage to go to Pilate when the last Jew who went to Pilate had been sent to the cross. He is in possession of a fresh-hewn tomb. Unless he was in the burial business as a profession, one has to assume he gave to Jesus a tomb he had earmarked for himself. He is prepared to make himself unclean by touching a dead body shortly before the Sabbath. He gives the body dignity. It is a fine thing to do.

Only one item in the account strikes the reader as odd. Luke has vividly described the tumultuous trial of Jesus before the council. He describes the council as made up of chief priests and scribes. Two questions are asked – "Are you the Messiah?" and "Are you the Son of God?" – and Jesus makes equivocal answers to both. The council members require no further testimony and bring him straight to Pilate (22.66–71). There is no mention of any dissent amongst the council. If Joseph of Arimathea really believed in Jesus, why did he not speak when it mattered? To take the body is a noble thing, but is it not too little, too late? What use is a disciple by night who has not the courage to be a disciple by day?

Mark

It was Preparation Day (that is, the day before the Sab-bath). So as evening approached, Joseph of Arimathea, a prominent member of the Council, who was himself waiting for the kingdom of God, went boldly to Pilate and asked for Jesus' body. Pilate was surprised to hear that he was already dead. Summoning the centurion, he asked him if Jesus had already died. When he learned from the centurion that it was so, he gave the body to Joseph. So

Joseph bought some linen cloth, took down the body, wrapped it in the linen, and placed it in a tomb cut out of rock. Then he rolled a stone against the entrance of the tomb. Mary Magdalene and Mary the mother of Joseph saw where he was laid. (15.42 – 47)

Mark's account is similar to Matthew's and Luke's, but it offers two additional words that make Joseph's role rather more ambivalent. The first word is "prominent": Joseph was a prominent member of the council. This exacerbates the issue we noted in Luke's account. Joseph was not only *present* at Jesus' trial and condemnation; he was *prominent*! Fewer than twenty-four hours later he steps forward to bury Jesus' body. Is this because he is a disciple on the quiet – "waiting for the kingdom of God" as Mark here records? If so, why was he so complicit in Jesus' condemnation? Perhaps there is a more cynical explanation – that Joseph, a prominent member of the council, stepped forward to put Jesus safely out of the public eye. He rolled a stone against the entrance of the tomb, and in order to keep the Jewish Law he completed the procedure before the Sabbath – mentioned explicitly at the beginning of this episode and a regular source of controversy in Jesus' ministry.

The second ambivalent word is "boldly". This only heightens the humiliation of the Jerusalem leadership in the process of Jesus' death. Joseph is a prominent member of the council, but even he has to summon up extreme courage to approach the Roman governor to complete the ugly business of disposing of an executed body.

The mitigating detail is that Mark's account, unlike the others, reintroduces the centurion at this point. The centurion is the executioner who at the moment of Jesus' death announced that this was truly God's Son (Mark 15.39). In doing so he identifies with the opening line of Mark's gospel – "the good news about Jesus the Messiah" (1.1). The centurion and Joseph are therefore both deeply compromised characters who ironically proclaim the gospel in word and deed at a moment when Jesus' regular disciples are invisible.

John

> Later, Joseph of Arimathea asked Pilate for the body of Jesus. Now Joseph was a disciple of Jesus, but secretly because he feared the Jewish leaders. With Pilate's permission, he came and took the body away. He was accompanied by Nicodemus, the man who earlier had visited Jesus at night. Nicodemus brought a mixture of myrrh and aloes, about seventy-five pounds. Taking Jesus' body, the two of them wrapped it, with the spices, in strips of linen. This was in accordance with Jewish burial customs. At the place where Jesus was crucified, there was a garden, and in the garden a new tomb, in which no one had ever been laid. Because it was the Jewish day of Preparation and since the tomb was nearby, they laid Jesus there. (19.38–42)

John's account of Jesus' burial includes two more details, which complicate matters further. One is that Jesus was buried with seventy-five pounds of myrrh and aloes. This is an incredible quantity. It takes the reader back to Mary's action in Bethany, where she took a pound of pure nard, worth 300 denarii according to Judas, and anointed Jesus' feet, wiping them with her hair (John 12.3–5). If Mary was so roundly criticized for using one pound to anoint Jesus, what are we to make of the use of seventy-five pounds? It is a colossal amount.

What does this enormous quantity mean? Three things come to mind, none of which reflect especially well on those burying Jesus. It could mean that two men who had been complicit in Jesus' condemnation and therefore execution, and yet were "secret disciples", were making an overwhelming gesture to represent their sense of guilt and desire to make amends. However it is hard to see how such a massive quantity of spices could have been both assembled and transported in so short a time – this is a period of no more than a few hours. So might the spices have been purchased and made ready ahead of time? Is there a rather sinister sense that those burying Jesus anticipated this situation and were sure to have the right equipment ready? Both of these theories seem flawed. Either way, the vast collection of spices tells us one thing: those burying Jesus expected his body to be there for a very long time. These are not people who held out any hope of resurrection.

Besides the quantity of spices, the striking feature of John's account is that Joseph of Arimathea is not the only secret disciple. He is joined by another, Nicodemus. And this is a man who has appeared before in John's gospel, not once but twice. It is time to consider this figure in his own right.

NICODEMUS

John's gospel does not make such subtle distinctions as the other gospels make between the kinds of people who were in charge in Jerusalem at the time of Jesus' ministry. Perhaps because this gospel was written somewhat later than the others, at a time when Pharisaism was the principal form of Judaism in the face of Roman dominance, John simply sees Pharisees as rulers. Nicodemus is a Pharisee – and therefore a leader. He comes to Jesus "by night".

Now there was a Pharisee, a man named Nicodemus who was a member of the Jewish ruling council. He came to Jesus at night and said, "Rabbi, we know that you are a teacher who has come from God. For no one could perform the signs you are doing if God were not with him." Jesus replied, "Very truly I tell you, no one can see the kingdom of God without being born again." "How can anyone be born when they are old?" Nicodemus asked. "Surely they cannot enter a second time into their mother's womb to be born!" Jesus answered, "Very truly I tell you, no one can enter the kingdom of God without being born of water and the Spirit. Flesh gives birth to flesh, but the Spirit gives birth to spirit. You should not be surprised at my saying, 'You must be born again.' The wind blows wherever it pleases. You hear its sound, but you cannot tell where it comes from or where it is going. So it is with everyone born of the Spirit." "How can this be?" Nicodemus asked. "You are Israel's teacher," said Jesus, "and do you not understand these things? Very truly I tell you, we speak of what we know, and we testify to what we have seen, but still you people do not accept our testimony. I have spoken to you of earthly things and you do not believe; how then will you believe if I speak of heavenly things? No one has ever gone into heaven except the one who came from heaven – the Son of Man. Just as Moses lifted up the snake in the wilderness, so the Son of Man must be lifted up, that everyone who believes may have eternal life in him." (3.1 – 15)

This is the first of two opportunities Nicodemus is given to choose between worldly respect, influence, and power on the one hand and true discipleship on the other. Things do not start auspiciously. Nicodemus is a Pharisee, of the party that gave John the Baptist a hard time in the wilderness; he is a member of the Sanhedrin, and therefore in Rome's pocket; and he comes by night; in other words in a personal, rather than an official, capacity. But he calls Jesus "Rabbi", so he suggests he could become a disciple.

Nicodemus cannot quite bring himself to consider his own discipleship, but he continues to talk of "we" – "we know that you are a teacher." John notes in 2.23 that "many people saw the signs he was performing and believed in his name"; here Nicodemus suggests he may be one of those people. But Jesus says discipleship is not about the signs. It is about a choice between God's rule and the current regime. It is not just an external thing. You have to be reborn. When Jesus adds the words "water and the Spirit", he is clearly talking about baptism. And not baptism in a quiet, private ceremony but baptism as a public act of witness.

Nicodemus chooses a delaying tactic: a question about human birth and conventional regeneration. But Jesus says it comes down to a choice between the flesh – the commitments Nicodemus currently has to power, wealth, and prestige – or the Spirit – the life that Jesus offers. But you cannot have the latter "by night", on the quiet. You cannot control it – it blows where it pleases. Nicodemus is facing up to the fact that if he follows Jesus, his life will get out of control. He will jeopardize everything he has worked so hard to secure: property, authority, influence. This is out of the question. It is as absurd as an old man reentering his mother's womb. Nicodemus is "Israel's teacher", but he has nothing to say in the face of this rabbi.

But later in the story, we have a chance to discover whether he has been decisively shaped by his encounter with Jesus. John 7 is set at the Feast of Tabernacles. Jesus appears in the temple courts halfway through the festival, creating a tumult. Faced with taunting that their inaction suggests their belief in Jesus, the Pharisees send a cohort of temple guards to arrest him. The guards return empty-handed, as this passage explains:

> Finally the temple guards went back to the chief priests and the Pharisees, who asked them, "Why didn't you bring him in?" "No one ever spoke the way this man does," the guards replied. "You mean he has deceived you also?" the Pharisees retorted. "Have any of the rulers or of the Pharisees believed in him? No! But this mob that knows nothing of the law – there is a curse on them." Nicodemus, who had gone to Jesus earlier and who was one of their own number, asked, "Does our law condemn a man without first hearing him to find out what he has been doing?" They replied, "Are you from Galilee, too? Look into it, and you will find that a prophet does not come out of Galilee." (7.45 – 52)

The guards play a role in this passage a little like the centurion's part in Mark's and Matthew's accounts of the crucifixion. In spite of themselves, they witness to the truth of Christ. Their change of heart leads to the Pharisees' telling question, "Have any of the rulers or of the Pharisees believed in him?" On the face of it this looks like a rhetorical question, and the answer is, "Of course not". But it turns out Nicodemus is there. Prefiguring his role in the trial and condemnation of Jesus, Nicodemus must have been present when the Pharisees decided to arrest Jesus by sending the temple guards; yet it seems he said nothing. Now he speaks – a little late, perhaps, but to the point: "Does our law condemn a man without first hearing him to find out what he has been doing?" Just as he does later in the story, Nicodemus does the right thing at the wrong time. At Jesus' death Nicodemus offers a worthy burial but fails to speak up for timely justice. Here he offers tardy justice but fails to speak up for due process. On neither occasion does he proclaim himself a public disciple.

Wes Howard-Brook offers a helpful reflection on Nicodemus's conduct at this point.

> His question presumes the basic validity of the system of law upon which Israel … [is] grounded. If "our Law" were applied properly, he claims, we would give this absent accusee full rights to confront his accusers, testify on his own behalf, explain his motives, and so on.… Many, many well-meaning but naïve protestors have found themselves in a U.S. courtroom hoping that if only their "rights" were respected, justice would emerge. I myself have been one of these, raised on the tradition of the 1960s that expected that if "good people" filled the judicial seats and the legislative bodies, the U.S. Constitution would allow for the development of just policies for all people. Thus, we as a nation passed civil rights laws to protect and provide equal opportunity for people of color, women, youth, elderly, and other marginalized persons. However, the experience of subsequent decades put the lie to change through the "liberal" route of assuring equal rights under law.…
>
> Nicodemus hopes that the precious and beloved Law that he appeals to as "ours" will be enough to vindicate Jesus without Nicodemus' personal witness. It is not.[3]

The Pharisees say to Nicodemus, "Are you from Galilee, too?" This is an ironic question in three senses. The first is that the Pharisees are referring to Galileans as uncouth, illiterate northerners. It does not occur to them that Nicodemus could be one of them, so he does not need to reply. The second is that now Nicodemus is being asked the questions. When Nicodemus was with

Jesus, Nicodemus was in the more comfortable role of asking the questions himself. The third is that this question anticipates the questions asked of Peter in the courtyard while Jesus' trial is being conducted – with Nicodemus present – in the high priest's house. Peter denies. Nicodemus merely remains silent. Both betray.

Thus Nicodemus, a figure who appears only in John's gospel, and Joseph of Arimathea are very similar characters. They together represent the four Gospels' ambivalence about whether discipleship can coexist with wealth, privilege, and power. Such people can make important contributions to the gospel story, becoming visible at just the point when the regular disciples are invisible. But it seems they appear only at the evening hour, once their "work", their public role, is done. They may have a personal faith, but, with the exception of their actions of Good Friday evening, it is not clear how that personal faith makes a public difference. The question remains: can one be a Christian "by night"?

CHRISTIANITY "BY NIGHT"?

We saw in chapter 1 that Jesus was put to death because he threatened to be more powerful than Rome. Jesus does not renounce power. Instead he represents power of a different kind from that which Pilate could comprehend. His is the power at the heart of creation, the axis of history, the grain of the universe. The second chapter, concerning Barabbas, demonstrated that Jesus' power did not rest on the use of violence. Jesus renounces violence because he has power. The weapons of war are rejected not because they are too powerful but because they are too weak; not because they change too much but because they change too little. And yet Jesus expects of his followers just as much commitment as the Zealots expect of theirs. Those who wish to be his followers must deny themselves, take up their cross, and follow him.

This third chapter, concerning Joseph of Arimathea and Nicodemus, observes two characters who fall between the power of Pilate and the passion of Barabbas. On the one hand, they are anxious to maintain their wealth, influence, and social prominence – all of which they owe to the political stranglehold maintained by the Roman governor. On the other hand, they are drawn by the figure from Nazareth and live in the shadow of the Galilean. They fear the consequences of throwing in their lot with the rabble, as vividly portrayed in Nicodemus's reticence at the Feast of Tabernacles in John 7. And so they are paralyzed, unable to play any active role in Jesus' passion, indeed complicit as members of the council in his condemnation and death. Only after Jesus has breathed his last do they appear, once again by night, and perform a noble service. What kind of discipleship is this?

It is a discipleship with which every reader of this book will be very familiar. Let me give four examples. In the modern professional culture, Christianity is not particularly respectable. It is widely assumed that Christianity is anti-intellectual in the sense that its adherents seem to be impervious to the discoveries of scientific and historical research and thus do not play by professional "rules". Moreover Christians are taken to have a conservative moral outlook that is assumed to fly in the face of the contemporary commitment to diversity and plurality of identity and self-expression. Professions emphasize the ability to carry out appropriate roles which require one to put one's own preferences and assumptions to one side; businesses require every conversation to return eventually to the bottom line of profit and loss. To cap it all, Christianity is still perceived as clinging to a constitutional or equivalent cultural role that entitles it to impose its views on others, which brings it into conflict with the pervasive cultural longing to be free of constraining obscurantism. When almost every product – cars, life insurance policies, even sanitary devices – is marketed on the appeal that it makes one free, Christianity is invariably portrayed as absurdly constraining. Even in circumstances when these and similar portrayals of Christianity are unjustified or even laughable, being a Christian in a business or professional culture sometimes takes courage and a thick skin.

So how is it to be done? It is understandable that some should feel the need to be Christians by night. To be a Christian by day means to be regarded as a dinosaur – dangerous and clumsy, deeply stupid, and a thing of the past. To avoid such a designation – and the stagnation to one's career it is likely to bring – one might well restrict one's discipleship to quiet, albeit generous, gestures in the darkness: a gift to a scholarship fund for overseas professional students perhaps, or a shadowy appearance at a company carol service. But the heart of professional life lies in discussions about whether the profession actually has a heart or whether it is just a slot machine for those with money to acquire skills and services. And most businesses and professions provide at least some opportunities to participate in a genuine strategic discussion – opportunities for Christians to dispel the notion that affirming Christians' identity means suppressing or oppressing other identities. These are times when people who have some influence in the organization (acquired by the quality of their work as much as by their seniority) get a chance to wonder out loud whether power is an end in itself or whether it should be used to set people free – by paying them a decent wage, or paying attention to their working environment, or assisting their educational or personal development, or encouraging them in facing the great questions of life and faith.

The business or professional person who is a Christian is a Christian by day when he or she ceases to regard Christianity as a set of ideas and begins to describe it as a set of practices (prayer,

Scripture reading, baptism, Eucharist, reconciliation, footwashing, visiting the sick, and so on) undertaken by faithful communities. These Christian practices should challenge the business or profession to assess whether it has its own faithful practices and whether, like the Christian ones, they yield truth and discipline and wisdom and honor. If not, it is time to work on them.

To take another example, the Christian minister, priest, or pastor may also find him or herself becoming a Christian by night. While much of the world in which he or she lives may resemble the world of business or the professions, and thus is a place where Christianity is in danger of becoming invisible, some of the world is very different. In rural communities, the priest is generally a welcome figure, affirming community when a sense of sustainable corporate life is perpetually under threat. In dislocated communities, including some inner cities and outer-urban housing estates or projects, the pastor is sometimes an honest broker between the "suits" and the "streets", a person who can speak both languages and be trusted by most if not all. In traditional communities, where the yearly cycle of festivals is valued not just for nostalgia but for opportunities to affirm family and friendship and fellowship and faith, and where the church's role in education is seen as an asset rather than as a threat, the minister can herald an opportunity for celebration. And in corridors of power, where moral seriousness is sometimes the casualty of urgency or ambition, public spin or private compromise, the lofty cleric who can say grace at the grand meal may yet stay to hear confession in the gentlemen's cloakroom.

What sense does it make to call these time-honored forms of Christian discipleship "by night"? Having experienced all of these forms of ministry, I know how much pressure there is to maintain one's presence by avoiding one's identity – in other words to be cheerful and positive without ever seriously articulating the story of Christ's birth, death, and resurrection, his calling to sacrificial discipleship, or his sending of the empowering Spirit. There is a pressure in many such contexts to recognize how much of a struggle life is for so many and thus not to introduce the news of Christ because it may leave some feeling bad. I recall a colleague on one management board on which I sat asking me not to wear a clerical collar at the board meetings. I explored over the subsequent months why it was that she and others felt uncomfortable with my appearing there as a priest. I came to the conclusion that a significant number of my colleagues, perhaps a majority, did not want a priest on the board; they were prepared to tolerate me there because they knew me as an individual and a friend, but they really did not want the church to be involved in any significant way. The discovery led to my deciding that for me to continue to say that my community needed me to be a priest – rather than a community worker – I needed to step down from that board. I was being pushed into being a Christian by night.

Moving to a third example, perhaps the most difficult place to be "outed" as a Christian in today's society is school. When adults discuss or contend over transcendent or moral claims, they have some kind of curriculum vitae to appeal to: "this is what I have done, this is what I have learned, these are the truths I have found to be evident." A teenager has little or no such record to appeal to. There is of course the appeal to the wisdom of the older sibling, parent, or teacher, but in the tension of the moment and intensity of peer pressure, little can substitute for self-possession and stout friendships. Well may high school students become Christians by night, slipping in late to class after an early Ash Wednesday service, slipping out early from class for an eagerly anticipated youth weekend away. Well may such students fear as deeply as Nicodemus the penetrating question, "Are you from Galilee, too?" Their wealth (such as it is) may not be in jeopardy, but their prestige and influence, their appeal in the sexual eyeing-up, and their ability to fit in with the crowd may plummet. If some, perhaps many, decide the only path of integrity in a world terrified of hypocrisy is to become Christians not even by night, in other words not at all, it is hardly surprising.

The fourth example must be known by every Christian. It is that of being a Christian in one's own family. This is perhaps more a question of the difficulty of being a Christian by night when one is a disciple by day. The sternest street protestor is shy of seeming judgemental before his or her own children. The greatest preacher fears seeming pious before his or her own household. Sometimes, sadly, the most compassionate pastor is a heartless or even brutal companion by night. And it is not just a matter of natural reticence or moral inconsistency. What of the person who becomes a Christian when his or her family is from another religion? When "My father will kill me" is not just a figure of speech? Those who are surrounded by like-minded people must be wary of judging too harshly those for whom being a Christian is a daily dance with danger, as it was for Joseph of Arimathea and for Nicodemus.

Joseph and Nicodemus are, perhaps, the ones Jesus had in mind when he told the story of the third slave who buried his talent in the ground (Matt. 25.18). For them, faith in Christ is not a matter of transformed identity – baptism – but is an attribute they can pick up or put down as they choose. As political figures, they are largely invisible, since when the key debates take place they are present but – at best – silent. As religious figures, they are visible at the very moment when the regular disciples have disappeared – the moment of Jesus' burial. They are celebrated religious figures, but they expose the politics of those who could have been political but chose to be narrowly religious. It is a politics that shows reverence to Jesus' body. But on closer inspection it is a politics that puts Jesus to death.

OPPORTUNITIES FOR INDIVIDUAL
OR GROUP REFLECTION

I wonder what are the simplest things Christians do.

I wonder what it is like to love someone who is being killed and yet say nothing.

I wonder what it is like to be on a committee or council and realize that others in the group are plotting something terrible.

I wonder what it is like to have someone look at you and say, "Are you one of them, too?"

I wonder what it would be like if "good people" filled all the seats in government and the judiciary.

I wonder what it is like to feel your personal faith makes no public difference.

I wonder what it is like to be a Christian in a business or factory.

I wonder what it is like to find that people despise you when they discover you are a Christian.

I wonder what it is like to talk with your family about your faith.

I wonder who we are protecting when we say faith is a private matter.

God of light and truth,
whose Son's forsaken body
was laid to rest by shadowy hands,
we pray for those who struggle to perceive
how their personal faith makes a public difference:
we bring before you those in business or factory or school
who fear the question, "Are you from Galilee too?";
those who find that the need to be accepted
precludes the call to witness to you and your kingdom;
and those for whom allegiance to your name
entails a secrecy in the face of danger.

Give us grace to follow the logic of straightforward actions,
like taking, wrapping, placing, cutting, rolling, and going
    away,
or taking, blessing, breaking, and giving.
Help us to hold on to the simplicity of discipleship,
so that when we go into the long night of temptation
    and fear,
we may walk in innocence and faithfulness,
telling the truth, loving mercy, listening for your voice,
and in the morning find we have walked humbly
with your Son, our God. Amen.

CHAPTER 4

MRS PILATE

The passion narrative is full of bit-part characters with walk-on roles, such as Simon of Cyrene, who carries Jesus' cross, the young man who runs away naked, and the thieves who berate and honor Jesus as they are crucified on either side of him. One of the most fascinating of these characters is Pilate's wife. She appears in only one verse in the Bible, but it is a verse full of resonance.

> While Pilate was sitting on the judge's seat, his wife sent him this message: "Don't have anything to do with that innocent man, for I have suffered a great deal today in a dream because of him." (Matt. 27.19)

Because the story tells us much less about Mrs Pilate than it does about the other characters in this book, the shape of this chapter will be different from the others. But it will still focus on the politics represented by what the gospel tells us about her. There is a difference between fruitful speculation and idle speculation. I shall take up four themes evoked by this short insight into the domestic life of the Pilates.

DREAMS

Not only is Mrs Pilate a dreamer, but she also suffers greatly in her dreams. There are four dimensions to the significance of her dream: its role in the story, its relationship to other dreams in Matthew's gospel, its connection to other dreams in the Bible, and the way it locates dreams in relation to issues of power and powerlessness.

In relation to the immediate story of Jesus' trial and crucifixion, Mrs Pilate's news creates a dramatic pause in the breathless sequence of events hurtling toward Jesus' execution. One of the most famous stories in the ancient world was the death of Julius Caesar at the hands of his trusted friend Brutus, and the celebrated account of Caesar's death is marked by Caesar's wife's having a fateful dream the previous night. This sets Jesus' death in the greatest available contemporary context. Mrs Pilate's dream gives some context to Pilate's actions in washing his hands a few verses later in the story. She has said, "Let there be nothing between you and this man", and Pilate, as we saw in chapter 1, seeks to portray himself as innocent of Jesus' blood.

Saint Augustine saw Pilate's wife as a contrast to Eve: Eve persuaded her husband to make a choice that led to death; Mrs Pilate pleaded with her husband to make a choice that would lead to life. Two other Old Testament wives may have a bearing on the portrayal of Mrs Pilate. Potiphar's wife is a less positive character who seeks to use her position as the consort of an influential man to gain the sexual favors of one of his slaves. That slave, Joseph, is in many ways a Christlike figure in the Genesis story, and he behaves with exemplary dignity in the face of duplicity. Another Old Testament character is Haman's wife, who appears in the book of Esther. Her name is Zeresh. Haman is a senior official in King Xerxes' Persian government, but however successful he becomes, he is constantly uneasy because of his antagonism with his Jewish rival Mordecai. Zeresh tells him to erect a gallows on which he can tell the king to hang Mordecai (Est. 5.14). (In fact it is Haman himself who dies on the gallows set up for Mordecai.) Just as the parallel to Caesar's wife's dream sets the trial of Jesus against a large-scale backdrop, so the contrast of Mrs Pilate with Eve, Mrs Potiphar, and Zeresh points to the unique significance of Jesus, which it seems even a potentially hostile Gentile cannot fail to recognize.

The second dimension to the significance of Mrs Pilate's dream comes in its relation to other dreams in Matthew's gospel, of which there are five. All of these dreams are part of the birth narrative. All but one involve Joseph. Joseph is told in a dream that Mary's son is conceived from the Holy Spirit and is to be named Jesus (Matt. 1.20–21); he is warned of Herod's murderous intentions and told to take his family to Egypt (Matt. 2.13); he is instructed to return to Israel after Herod's death (Matt. 2.19–20); and he is warned that Herod's son Archelaus is ruling in Judea, and instead he settles in Nazareth in Galilee (Matt. 2.22–23). In between the first dream and the last three, there is one further dream. This comes to the magi, who are warned not to return to Herod, and thus they leave Bethlehem for their own country without going back to Jerusalem (Matt. 2.12). There is no doubt in any of these dreams that God is communicating directly with the dreamer. There is no ambiguity. These dreams require no interpretation. Thus one is led to suppose that Mrs Pilate's dream is of the same kind.

It is significant that both Mrs Pilate and the magi are Gentiles. God is communicating directly with people who do not have the Jewish Scriptures as their regular guide to God's ways. In the first story, the magi, who are Gentiles but are listening attentively to the God of Israel, are contrasted sharply with the Jerusalem leaders, who, though Jews, are eager to dispose of God's only Son. In the second story a similar cast of Jerusalem characters reappears with equal appetite for Jesus' death, and they are contrasted with Mrs Pilate, again a Gentile who not only perceives Jesus' righteousness (on what may have been minimal exposure to him) but also acts on that revelation in a way few other characters in the narrative do. If Mrs Pilate's insight and openness to revelation look back to the Gentile magi at the outset of the gospel, they also look forward from the moment of Jesus' sentencing to the moment of his death, when the centurion, another Gentile, declares that this was truly God's Son (Matt. 27.54). Jesus' righteousness is evident to Gentiles on even small acquaintance, but those in authority in Jerusalem cannot – or will not – see it.

The third dimension is the relationship of Mrs Pilate's dream to dreams in the Bible as a whole. The Old Testament has broadly two kinds of dreams. There are message dreams, in which God appears to the dreamer and delivers a message. For example, Jacob dreams of a ladder of angels ascending to and descending from heaven (Gen. 28.12–15); God then tells him, "I will give you and your descendants the land on which you are lying ... All peoples on earth will be blessed through you and your offspring" (28.13–14). And there are symbolic dreams, in which God does not appear, but the dreamer sees images that generally need interpretation (most famously, Pharaoh's dreams about the seven fat and seven thin cows and the seven healthy and seven scorched heads of grain in Genesis 41.1–7). Of the first type, the message dreams, there are broadly three kinds: dreams that speak of God's promises to his chosen servants and their descendants, dreams that are received in holy places, and warning dreams.

Interestingly, warning dreams come only to Gentiles. God appears to Abimelek, king of Gerar, after he has taken Sarah, Abraham's wife, and says, "You are as good as dead because of the woman you have taken; she is a married woman." Abimelek protests and says Abraham called Sarah his sister. God says, "That is why I did not let you touch her. Now return the man's wife, for he is a prophet, and he will pray for you and you will live. But if you do not return her, you may be sure that you and all who belong to you will die" (Gen. 20.1–7). Later God appears to Laban. Jacob has run away with his two wives, Rachel and Leah, Laban's daughters, and Laban is in hot pursuit. But God says to Laban, "Be careful not to say anything to Jacob, either good or bad" (Gen. 31.24). Mrs Pilate's dream appears to be another dream of this kind. It comes to a Gentile and thus affirms God's purpose across all peoples. It warns of an action that might bring untold calamity upon the perpetrator. And it identifies God's chosen instrument – whether Abraham, Jacob, or in this case Jesus – who is the main concern of the story. Mrs Pilate may be a minor character, but she takes her place in an honored tradition.

The fourth dimension of Mrs Pilate's dream is the most pertinent to the theme of this book. Dreams have an important role to play in relation to power and powerlessness. Joseph and Daniel are both characters that bear significant resemblances to Jesus as he is portrayed in the passion narrative. Joseph has a dream that makes him very unpopular. Like with Jesus, those close to Joseph, who might have been expected to cherish him, in fact conspire against him. Israel's journey down into Egypt and up into the Promised Land anticipates Jesus' going down into death and the grave and up into resurrection and new life. Joseph's cistern, into which his brothers threw him (Gen. 37.24), and Daniel's den of lions, into which the royal administrators, prefects, satraps, advisers, and governors of the Persian Empire hurled him (Dan. 6.16), are both "types" of Jesus' grave. When Joseph and Daniel emerge from below, they demonstrate God's power to bring good out of even the worst evil. In that sense both Joseph and Daniel die and rise again.

Joseph and Daniel understand the power of dreams. Dreams in the Bible are an inbreaking of God's future into the unpromising circumstances of the present. They unsettle the proud – men such as Pharaoh in the Joseph story, Nebuchadnezzar in the Daniel story, and Pilate in Matthew's gospel. They vindicate God's chosen – Abraham, Jacob, Jesus. They involve even Gentiles in the discovery of God's strange but relentless providence – Abimelek, Laban, Mrs Pilate. And yet they do not coerce, destroy, or manipulate. They simply draw back the veil between earth and heaven, disclosing the purpose of God and the mysterious ways God's purpose takes shape in the lives of his people. For the powerful, dreams are something to fear, but for the powerless, dreams are a point of contact with the place where true power lies.

Many people find the subject of dreams embarrassing. Since Freud, dreams have become associated with the subconscious, with sublimated desires, and particularly with suppressed sexual urges. But the stories of the Old and New Testaments do not assume that dreams are primarily about us. They assume that dreams are primarily about God. In dreams, through explicit message or intriguing symbol, people become aware of the surprising ways in which God keeps his story alive. Dreams are especially significant for those – like Joseph – for whom all seems lost and for those – like the magi – who would otherwise have no particular reason to discover the God of Abraham. They are a way in which God communicates with us when adversity or affluence would otherwise blind us to his work. They are a way in which God's power infuses our human passion.

THE WIFE OF THE GOVERNOR

The verse in Matthew is the only mention of Mrs Pilate in classical literature. There are a number of references to Pontius

Pilate before and after his encounter with Jesus, but there is no other word about his wife. We do not even know whether she accompanied him to Judea; it was not common for wives to join their husbands on commissions such as this, but Matthew's account makes little sense if she did not, given that a message would have taken weeks to reach Jerusalem from Rome.

Thus speculating on Mrs Pilate's character and political significance is more a matter of imagination than research. But it is nonetheless valuable for that. Here are four scenarios that may provoke the imagination into the power and the powerlessness of the governor's wife.

Claudia is a highly intelligent, artful person who realized at an early age that the only way she would gain power and influence would be to attach herself to an upwardly mobile man. She is fond of her husband, but they both know that being a domestic goddess hardly makes her heart sing. In the early days she used to help him write some of his speeches and prepare for some of the great debates of his career. But as he gathered more staff and hangers-on to do this for him, Claudia found much less of a role in his life. She is expected by many to play the perfect hostess, but she finds the small talk required for endless receptions very tiresome. She knows that in many ways she makes her husband feel small; successful as he is, they both know that she is the real brains of the operation. She has her suspicions that he has been more than tempted to take comfort in the arms of women who pose less of an intellectual and emotional challenge to him. She is under no such illusion that if she pursued another such relationship it would make her happy; beneath her own desire for mental challenge and discovery lies a profound sense of duty and honor and an abiding conviction in the dignity of Rome. She is no longer much in the habit of advising her husband on policy matters, but she has had a dream that has unsettled her deeply. A part of her hopes that an intimate communication with her husband will restore his sense that she cares about his success and that she does not secretly despise him. But she doubts he will take any notice; his advisers will look after that.

Julia is an elegant woman who at an early age got so used to the power over men her looks gave her that it seemed natural to use her power to secure the most famous husband available. She is not without skill and craft and has proved an adept mother to seven children. She is beginning to wonder what social skills she will need to develop for the time when her striking looks can no longer bring her the rewards she seeks. While she maintains a civil relationship with her husband, her real energy goes into her intense friendships with a variety of socially voracious society women in Rome. She enjoys all the benefits of having a powerful husband without the need to spend too much time with him; his work is lucrative, and her facility to spend money is considerable. However for curiosity's sake she decides to take a trip to Judea to see this land that keeps her husband's whole attention. While in this strange province, she hears stories about a prophet from Nazareth. On one occasion, while she is walking through Jerusalem, she sees him, and when he turns to face her, his gaze goes straight through her. She cannot forget this gaze. She begins to ask herself questions about who she is and who he is. She has a profound dream about him, about how he will return to judge the Romans for their oppression. And then she wakes up and finds he has been arrested. She is panic stricken. She sends a message to her husband, pleading with him to take this man seriously; but she knows he will not understand the message, since it is so unlike any she has ever sent him before.

Lydia is a gentle, careful person who deeply loves her husband. She was deeply flattered when a young man who was clearly destined for public office sought her out and proposed marriage to her. She has never sought a role in his public life, but she is used to him talking with her about the cares of his soul. She knows others see her as a powerful person because she is married to a provincial governor. But she sees only how difficult it is for her husband to bring his unruly province under his control, and how little real peace the *Pax Romana* is bringing to Judea. She has always sought to maintain a strict moral code for herself and her husband and family, but her husband is facing challenges that are beyond the scope of her largely domestic imagination. She sees him as the father of his province, but she is realizing that few of the populace see themselves as his children. She longs for her husband to be a successful governor, and she winces when he is forced to take brutal steps to keep the province in order. She is aware of a number of so-called prophets who become the focus of the people's aspirations, and among them she has been aware of one who seems to be antagonizing the Jerusalem authorities more than he is bothering her husband. One night she has a dream that for the first time brings her to see matters from the point of view of the occupied Jewish people. She sees this good and righteous man expressing everything that is noble about his people, and she sees him being tortured and executed. This execution seems to corrupt everything she believes the Roman Empire stands for: justice, peace, and dignity. She wakes up to find it is so and sends a message to plead with her husband to spare this man for the sake of the honor of Rome. For the first time she begins to wonder if she has been deceiving herself about the honor of Rome and her husband's role in what is beginning to feel like a charade.

Sylvia is a generous-hearted but shy person who married very young and has never had a chance to discover who she is other than as a wife to her rather older husband. She has always been very observant of her religious duties in relation to the gods of Rome. With her husband often away for long periods, and with his tending to be emotionally rather distant even when physically present, Sylvia has learned to develop her own spiritual resources. It is very hard to form friendships when your husband is such a prominent figure and holds the power of life and death over many of the people whom you meet, so Sylvia has explored the inner places of her soul in contemplation and meditation. When she spends an extended period in Judea, she comes to hear of the prophet from Nazareth, and she hears about the centurion whose servant Jesus healed. She secretly meets Jesus and finds in him a man who combines both a way and a life – both the inner healing she has tried to find through meditation and the outer truth she has always sought through the traditional Roman gods. She is transformed, such that even her husband notices. But she keeps her conversion a secret and finds ways to support the disciples financially from the large allowance her husband passes to her from his rich earnings from taxes and extortion. She is dismayed to hear that Jesus is in grave danger. It forces her to face the conflict between her outer life as a supporter of the Roman stranglehold on the province and her inner life as a devoted follower of the Galilean. All night after his arrest she tosses and turns in agony at his suffering and in dismay at her own. Finally she decides to tell her story to her husband and to plead with him to save this man on whom she believes not only her destiny but also his depends.

I hope both these imaginative reconstructions and this book as a whole make clear that it is too simplistic to think of a person as being either powerful or powerless. More fruitful is to examine how each of these designations applies.

Mrs Pilate is powerful in a number of ways. First, she is able to dream and to remember her dreams. As we have seen, dreams in the Bible tend to be ways in which God's future breaks into the narrative. To dream is therefore to be a person who is becoming aware of God's future. Since there is no power in the universe that compares to God's providence, the way God brings good out of evil and resurrection out of crucifixion, the power to dream is perhaps Mrs Pilate's greatest power.

Next, she has sexual power – the power to change the course of events by evoking attraction, lust, jealousy, and love and either ignoring, encouraging, teasing such feelings or rejecting them. Of course, men have similar powers, but we are talking here about a woman who was denied many of the outlets that were open to many of the men in her world. It is unwise to underestimate the power of saying to one's husband, "I have been dreaming about another man." One does not have to be Sigmund Freud to have some sense that dreams relate to some degree to unfulfilled desires. At the very least, for Mrs Pilate to say that she has been dreaming about Jesus suggests Jesus has caught her imagination to such an extent that she has become fascinated by him. Whether or not this is a sexual fascination is relatively unimportant. Many, perhaps most, married men would rather their wives were fascinated only by them. Many, perhaps most, married men who are aware that their wives are attractive in looks or in personality are not unaware that those qualities will make their wives attractive to other men. This can lead to pride and complacency at their "trophy" or "possession", or to deep anxiety and insecurity at their vulnerability in the face of rivals. Few things tickle the thrill of a playful or illicit relationship more than a furtive message delivered at a risky or inappropriate moment – think of the way email and text messaging shape the pace of romantic relationships today. How much more tantalizing, then, a message delivered to Pilate as he sits in judgement to say that his wife is captivated by the man he is poised to sentence to death? Imagine the irony of Pilate, a man seen as the focus of power in Jesus' trial, being manipulated by his wife's terse but intriguing hint of her fascination with the shadow of the Galilean. When leading public figures are discovered to have complex or disreputable sexual histories, one could make an urbane or a cynical response that perceives the misuse of power or the triumph of libido or the exposure of selfish duplicity. But a more charitable perspective would be to observe that even men who obtain widespread influence and authority and respect still have to find ways of resolving the many aspects of their desire, addressing whatever deep insecurities they may have and handling their own jealousies and rivalries – and that some manage these things more successfully than others. Much infidelity is less a pursuit of ecstasy and conquest and more a restless search for affirmation and security however misguided that search may be. How will Pilate react to being told he is not the only man on his wife's mind? It is an electric disclosure.

Third, there is the power of the word "innocent" – often translated "righteous". As I argued in chapter 1, the conventional portrayal of Pontius Pilate as a conscientious, honest broker surrounded by a gallery of hotheaded fanatics is an implausible one. Pilate had significant interests of his own, and all pointed in the direction of Jesus' execution. Except one. As we noted again in the first chapter, what mattered in Rome was not just power and wealth; it was also prestige. And prestige involved matters such as honor and dignity. Simply to rub out a profoundly good man for the cynical purpose of maintaining power and therefore wealth was not a desirable course of action. Those who sacrifice the moral high ground are usually looking for ways to claim it back in one way or another. Once Mrs Pilate talks about Jesus as an innocent, righteous man, she has poked her husband in the small of his back. It is not surprising he makes a display of washing his hands. It is a desperate attempt to persuade others – especially his wife – that he is acting with integrity.

Fourth, and most obviously, Mrs Pilate has access to considerable wealth and influence. The idea that she may have been one of the women who secretly supported Jesus is pure speculation – but the idea that she had access to the funds to be able to do so is not. Today those with wealth and power tend to be hedged about with the requirement of transparency, the legacy of audit trails, and the suspicion of conflicts of interest. For a wife or husband to have access to significant funds would be seen as unprofessional, perhaps criminal. But the Romans had no such strictures. Becoming a governor was a route to power and wealth because it gave one many ways to make money and exercise patronage. Mrs Pilate had access to as much money as she could possibly want, and if she had asked for "the head of John the Baptist" as Herodias did (Mark 6.24), she probably would not have had to employ the device of a seductive dancing daughter to get what she wanted.

Yet for all these aspects of power, Mrs Pilate may not have experienced her life as that of a powerful person. How could this be? It rather depends on what those things were that she really wanted. Four come to mind very easily.

It would be understandable if what she most wanted was the love of her husband. She would not be the first. How many women over the centuries have lived apparently desirable lives yet inside have known a gnawing despair that the one thing they craved was beyond their reach? What was driving Pilate? A whole host of desires for wealth and power and prestige? And could he not realize that these were all distractions from what mattered most? Did he not care for the woman whose support had given him his vital early confidence, whose love had restored him after one setback and then another, whose body had given him his precious children and heirs? If Mrs Pilate felt she could not reach her husband's heart, whether it was consumed with administration or adulation or adultery, well may she have felt powerless, for all her wealth and influence.

Expectations of what an able woman may expect to achieve have been transformed in recent decades, but it would still not be anachronistic to imagine that Mrs Pilate might have felt powerless in that she felt she had no life of her own. To be always defined by her husband, to be at the whim of the emperor and his entourage, to be at the mercy of the fall of the political dice, she must have felt vulnerable in a host of ways. She may well have been more able, more politically astute, more attractive and diplomatic than her husband, but there was no route to public office for her. She could be a society queen, a patron of the arts, a seductive hostess, or a noble consort; there were few other options. The scripts were already laid out for her. Well may she have felt trapped – and powerless.

If she aspired to dignity and honor for herself and her husband, again she may have felt powerless. This comes down to the issue raised at the end of chapter 1 and in the story of Lydia above: what if Mrs Pilate begins to realize that the foundations of the Roman Empire are not as grand and noble as she may have been brought up to suppose? Mrs Pilate finds herself caught up in a political system that she begins to see as hollow and corrupt. What can she do about it? Nothing. Not only is the regime profoundly disturbing, but even worse, she is publicly visible as a notable beneficiary of its abuses. This would be an almost unbearable tension for a person of integrity.

And finally, we know only one thing about what Mrs Pilate really wanted: she wanted Jesus spared. And we can see this as the culmination of the other things she may have wanted. If she could not have a life of her own, in which she could flourish and contribute to those forces in the empire that she wanted to enhance, then it was reasonable for her to seek two things: a life of integrity for her husband, in which his career charted a path she could take pride in and promoted that in which they both believed; and his unswerving love, seeking if not a constant physical and emotional desire, then at least an enriching acknowledgment of their creative interdependence. Asking for Jesus' life to be spared in such a dramatic manner was a test of these two things, a test of the two pillars on which her life depended. And the test failed.

A SECRET SUPPORTER OF JESUS?

I have given a sympathetic reading of Mrs Pilate that sees her as a person who, at least after her dream if not before, is "not far from the kingdom of God", to recall a line that Jesus uses in relation to the scribe who asked him about the greatest commandment. Since this chapter is almost entirely founded on speculation, I am going to take the liberty of a little more: could Mrs Pilate's dream have had the same effect on her that the magi's astronomy had on them? Could it have turned her into a secret believer? What might have been her reaction if and when she heard reports that Jesus' followers claimed he had risen from the dead?

In taking the imaginative reconstruction of the circumstances of Jesus' passion this far, I am seeking to paint Mrs Pilate as a counterpart to the figures discussed in the last chapter, Joseph of Arimathea and Nicodemus. These two men did have the opportunity to play a significant political role before Jesus died, but they appear to have chosen not to – whether through fear, lack of understanding, or lack of faith. Yet they play a significant religious role after Jesus' death – providing a grave and carrying out an appropriate burial. By contrast Mrs Pilate had little or no access to Jesus during his life and almost no ability to influence the forces that were at work at his trial. But she manages to make a contribution that, as we have seen, may have jeopardized the whole of her future life and well-being.

Her contribution and the possibility of her future faith calls to mind an intriguing and neglected passage in Luke's gospel:

After this, Jesus traveled about from one town and village to another, proclaiming the good news of the kingdom of God. The Twelve were with him, and also some women who had been cured of evil spirits and diseases: Mary (called Magdalene) from whom seven demons had come out; Joanna the wife of Chuza, the manager of Herod's household; Susanna; and many others. These women were helping to support them out of their own means. (8.1–3)

It is sometimes observed that the Gospels are written like medieval romance tales in that in a romance, no one ever enquires who pays for the hero's accommodation. Well, here is the answer. The disciples had secret backers. The most fascinating of them is "Joanna the wife of Chuza, the manager of Herod's household". This person seems to be the closest analogy to Mrs Pilate. Joanna is of course nothing like as prominent as the wife of the provincial governor, but Herod was nonetheless a significant figure, and the manager of his household would have been a person of some wealth and visibility. This account suggests that Jesus had healed her in some way; it is tantalizing not to have a description. (Those who suppose the evangelists created some or all of the healing accounts must explain why Luke has not therefore satisfied our desire for a story that tells us about Joanna's restoration and how her husband and his colleagues reacted.) It is hard to imagine that Joanna's husband, let alone his boss, would have countenanced her supporting Jesus and his disciples so explicitly.

If in the last chapter I was critical of those who seek to be disciples by night, here may be the place to see things from a different point of view. Joseph and Nicodemus were men; they were men of wealth and political influence; they had access both to Jesus and to those who sought Jesus' death. They could see which way events were heading, and they had some opportunity to stop matters from getting to the point they did. Mrs Pilate was different. She was a woman. She had a lot of access to her husband but little or none to the other decision-makers in the province. She was trapped in a way Joseph and Nicodemus were not. And yet she did a very remarkable thing.

If she were a secret follower – and we have no evidence, so this is just an exercise of constructive wondering – then I believe it is possible to draw some conclusions from her role in the story. One is that there may be a difference between being a secret follower – one who wishes to worship and follow Jesus but who is prevented from doing so – and being a disciple by night – one who has full exposure to the glory of the Lord but who chooses to see discipleship as a matter of religious observance separated from political commitment. Another is that these secret followers may crop up in the most unlikely of places. God speaks to the wife of the provincial governor. Imagine God speaking to Leonid Brezhnev's wife or to Deng Xiaoping's wife or to Nicolae Ceausescu's wife. Nothing is impossible with God. A third is that being a secret follower does not mean being an entirely silent follower. Mrs Pilate may have said little or nothing before – and even after – this crucial moment in history, but each follower, secret or visible, has a vital role to play in God's kingdom, and much or all of our lives are a preparation for that poignant moment. Jesus tells a parable about two sons:

> "There was a man who had two sons. He went to the first and said, 'Son, go and work today in the vineyard.' 'I will not,' he answered, but later he changed his mind and went. Then the father went to the other son and said the same thing. He answered, 'I will, sir,' but he did not go. Which of the two did what his father wanted?" "The first," they answered. (Matt. 21.28–31)

Perhaps Mrs Pilate is like the first son and the visible disciples more like the second. At the moment of truth, it was she who spoke up for Jesus.

SUFFERING A GREAT DEAL BECAUSE OF HIM

One final aspect of the very brief account of Mrs Pilate's intervention in the passion narrative is the fascinating expression "I have suffered a great deal today in a dream because of him." What does it mean to say she had suffered because of Jesus?

It takes Mrs Pilate into a very special category of Christlike people, those who can be said to have shared Christ's passion. In several places Paul talks in these terms. At the very end of his letter to the Galatians, Paul says, "From now on, let no one cause me trouble, for I bear on my body the marks of Jesus" (Gal. 6.17). Even more explicitly, in Colossians, Paul identifies with the passion of Christ, explaining how he shares in Christ's redeeming work: "Now I rejoice in what I am suffering for you, and I fill up in my flesh what is still lacking in regard to Christ's afflictions, for the sake of his body, which is the church" (Col. 1.24). More generally he speaks of his body as being the site of Christ's death and resurrection: "We always carry around in our body the death of Jesus, so that the life of Jesus may also be revealed in our body" (2 Cor. 4.10).

Can genuine suffering ever be regarded as an honor? Perhaps in such a very rare case as this. The negative side of Mrs Pilate's dream is perhaps that she suffers because she discovers who this man really is. Can she imagine that 2,000 years later (and no doubt long, long after that) her husband's name will be recalled as the man who oversaw the biggest catastrophe in all of history, a catastrophe that could have been avoided had he shown any true interest in honor, dignity, and nobility? Had she had even a glimpse of that, of course she would have suffered. If in addition she had perceived for the first time, or for the first time so clearly, that the rule over which her husband presided was empty, a vessel of violence containing no elixir of truth, and as a result her esteem for her husband and her own self-respect had plummeted, then again, undoubtedly, she would have suffered. And if she had always believed her husband did indeed love her and trust her judgement and deeply respect her, and yet she now realized that he would not take her imploring advice when it was delivered in a way it never had been before, surely she would have suffered, especially if it made her wonder whether her marriage was a house built on sand.

But perhaps the heart of her suffering was this. She had seen into the heart of goodness, the soul of truth, the veil of beauty; she had experienced a love beyond her imagination, a mercy so transforming and a healing so complete that she for the first time saw her previous monochromatic life for the pale shadow it had been. This was the living God, no doubt about it, and no risk, no venture, no demand was too great to respond to this joy that had come into her dreams, her mind, her whole life. And yet every one of her commitments was unsettled or potentially destroyed by this new discovery: her husband's role as provincial governor; her social role at the head of an oppressive social world strangling the life of the province; the very soul of the Roman Empire's role of proclaiming peace but only so long as peace served its acquisitiveness, bringing civilizing transport and coinage but only so long as it distributed soldiers and raised taxes, using emperor worship as a means of social control. Her suffering was that Jesus offered to transform her into a new creation, but every fiber of her body was locked into the old world. By begging her husband, she was begging for time; Jesus' crucifixion was forcing her to face her tragic position. Rich, perhaps beautiful, influential, and no doubt much admired, she was suffering a very private sorrow in her dreams, for she was trapped. Trapped by the power and the passion of Christ.

OPPORTUNITIES FOR INDIVIDUAL
OR GROUP REFLECTION

I wonder what it is like to feel one's dreams are more real than the rest of one's life.

I wonder whether God speaks to people in dreams today.

I wonder what it would feel like to be warned by God in a dream.

I wonder what it would be like to have an experience that seemed just like the experience of someone in the Bible.

I wonder what it is like for a woman to feel that she is much more able than her husband but that no one will ever know it.

I wonder what it is like for a woman to feel powerless when everyone sees her husband as powerful.

I wonder what it is like to feel there is no one you can trust.

I wonder what it is like to know the truth about somebody very close and not ever be able to tell anyone.

I wonder what it is like to feel that somebody one is close to is making a terrible mistake.

I wonder what it is like to suffer a great deal because of Christ.

I wonder what it is like not to be able to tell anyone about one's Christian faith.

God of love and gentleness,
whose Son, Jesus, was often recognized more quickly
    by strangers
than by many he called his own:
we pray for those whom others assume are powerful
but whose own experience is very different;
for those who feel trapped by public expectations or
    restrictive roles;
for those who long for the responsive love
of a partner, child, parent, or friend
on whom limitless attention has been shed;
for those whose care for a person in power has parted
    company
with their respect for the policies they are pursuing.

Help us to employ the power we have,
whether that power include sexuality, influence, access,
    or innocence,
in such a way that, hidden or secretive as we may need to be,
we can be prophets and bearers of good news
to those who walk in the valley of the shadow of death.

Be present to us through the silent hours of the night,
that we may dream,
and in our dreams encounter your kingdom, your destiny,
the company of the downtrodden who walk with you,
and most of all you yourself, made present through your
    Holy Spirit
in your Son, Jesus Christ. Amen.

CHAPTER 5

PETER

Peter appears in the Gospels more than any other character discussed in this book. But I shall limit my treatment of him to three key passages. The central passage is his threefold denial of Jesus, recorded in all four gospels. To get an idea of the catastrophe of that denial, I shall begin by recalling Peter's commissioning as the foundation of the church. And to get a sense of how Peter's denial is not just a catastrophe, I shall go on to consider Peter's recommissioning by Jesus as shepherd of his flock.

ON THIS ROCK

When Jesus came to the region of Caesarea Philippi, he asked his disciples, "Who do people say the Son of Man is?" They replied, "Some say John the Baptist; others say Elijah; and still others, Jeremiah or one of the prophets." "But what about you?" he asked. "Who do you say I am?" Simon Peter answered, "You are the Messiah, the Son of the living God." Jesus replied, "Blessed are you, Simon son of Jonah, for this was not revealed to you by flesh and blood, but by my Father in heaven. And I tell you that you are Peter, and on this rock I will build my church, and the gates of death will not overcome it. I will give you the keys of the kingdom of heaven; whatever you bind on earth will be bound in heaven, and whatever you loose on earth will be loosed in heaven." Then he ordered his disciples not to tell anyone that he was the Messiah.

From that time on Jesus began to explain to his disciples that he must go to Jerusalem and suffer many things at the hands of the elders, the chief priests and the teachers of the law, and that he must be killed and on the third day be raised to life. Peter took him aside and began to rebuke him. "Never, Lord!" he said. "This shall never happen to you!" Jesus turned and said to Peter, "Get behind me, Satan! You are a stumbling block to me; you do not have in mind the concerns of God, but merely human concerns." Then Jesus said to his disciples, "Whoever wants to be my disciple must deny themselves and take up their cross and follow me. For whoever wants to save their life will lose it, but whoever loses their life for me will find it." (Matt. 16.13–25)

The three conversations I am considering in this chapter take place in widely differing contexts. This first encounter is set on the edge. Jesus takes his disciples to the northern borderlands, to a place with a significant name. It was called Caesarea Philippi. The first part of the name was the name of the Roman emperor, Caesar, sometimes known as the living son of god, the self-styled savior, protector, and deliverer of his people. The second part is named after Philip, ruler of the region, lapsed Jew and puppet of the hated Romans. You may recall Philip's wife went off with his brother Herod Antipas, which led to the death of John the Baptist.

So the name Caesarea Philippi represents all that was wrong with the way Palestine was governed in Jesus' time. And the town was also, and still is, known as Banyas, after the Greek god Pan, who had a shrine there. So Jesus is on the border with the Gentiles, the border of Jewish faith and culture, and he is at the heart of the question of where authority lies in Israel.

Jesus turns and asks, "Who do people say that the Son of Man is?" And the disciples talk about John, Elijah, Jeremiah – all of them prophets who proclaimed repentance and judgement. "But who do *you* say that I am?" says Jesus. You can imagine the silence. Then Peter says, "You are the anointed king Israel has been waiting for for 500 years. You are the very presence of God among us. You are the one who will restore the intimate companionship of God and his people." And Jesus blesses Peter and says, "Peter, you didn't discover this for yourself – it was God who gave you the vision to see what you have seen and say what you have said."

Jesus announces that this is the moment, this is the place, and this is the conversation on which his church is to rest. You could call this quite a Genesis thing to do. God said to Abram, "I will make you the father of many nations", and promptly changed his name to Abraham, meaning ancestor of many. Later God fought with Jacob all night and then said, "You shall no longer be called Jacob but Israel, for you have striven with God and with humans and have prevailed." In just the same way, Jesus marks a new beginning for the people of God by giving a new and descriptive name, Peter, the rock. And the people founded on this rock are to be Jesus' own people, for he calls them *my* church. Jesus knows Peter is a willing but impetuous follower, who promises more than he delivers. He knows Peter is on occasion stupid, selfish, scared, and just plain wrong. But he nonetheless founds the church on him and promises that the forces of evil and death combined will never be stronger than this seemingly fragile rock.

Finally Jesus announces that he will give Peter the keys of God's empire, the swipe card to the universe. He will trust Peter with knowing when to constrain people and when to let them go, when to shape the church along the contours of human limitations and when to set people free to explore the boundless possibilities of life in the Spirit. Jesus tells the disciples to keep these secrets to themselves just for now, because they have not yet grasped that the cost of all this wonder and glory is the cross, and the cross is still way beyond their imaginations.

So that is what this story meant in the first century. Against the backdrop of pagan religion, Roman domination, and Jewish collaboration, Peter names Jesus as the embodiment of God's purposes for his people, and Jesus names Peter as the rock on which the new form of companionship with God will be founded. Peter says, "Israel, God's people, will never be the same again." Jesus says, "Neither will you, Peter."

So much for 2,000 years ago. What does this story mean for our contemporary culture? Well, let's start with the context. If the Caesar of Caesarea is those forces that dominate our lives while claiming to be our defender, our savior, the bringer of peace, then Caesar is all around us. If the Philip of Philippi is those institutions that epitomize the collapse of fine traditions and noble ideals into shoddy compromises and shameless backhanders, then Philippi is sadly no distant nightmare either. And Banyas, the shrine of Pan: surely we can see that we live today in a marketplace of faiths, torn between the credulity and inhumanity of fanaticism and the cynicism and despair of unbelief. We are all on the road to Caesarea Philippi.

In this context people still admire Jesus, whether as a controversial firebrand like John the Baptist or a miracle-working maverick like Elijah or a kill-joy doom-monger like Jeremiah. But the farther we get from the messianic expectation of the first century, the bigger Peter's claim about Jesus seems to become. Where Peter would have said "Jews", we would say "everyone". Where Peter might have said "people", we would say "all creation". Where Peter might have said "world", we would say "universe". Where Peter said, "You are the Messiah, the Son of the living God", we might say, "You are the epicenter of the universe, the purpose of creation, the meaning of existence, the bond that joins humanity to God forever."

If this is who Jesus is, we humans have no scientific or deductive capacity to identify him. Science largely works by mapping repeated phenomena, and Jesus is a one-off. So the evidence of Peter's five senses could not have told him who Jesus was because you can't recognize something if neither you nor anyone else has ever seen it before. This is a recognition that can come only from God: it is revelation.

If this story tells us exactly who Jesus is for us today, then it also tells us what the church is. The church is still Peter. That is, the church is a fragile people inspired by God to speak the truth about Jesus. Peter spoke the truth about Jesus; so does the church. But Peter was not infallible. Neither is the church. If Peter spoke the truth, it was because God inspired his words; so it is for the church. Peter was sometimes stupid, selfish, scared, and just plain wrong; so is the church. But Jesus chose Peter. And Jesus still chooses the church. Who are we to differ?

Fallible and clumsy it may sometimes be, but the church will never be overcome by death or evil. So long as it continues to live as a fragile people inspired by God to speak the truth about Jesus, the church will never be extinguished by evil or death. The best football matches leave the spectators on the edge of their seats till the last nail-biting minute, with the result in the balance. But reality isn't a football cliffhanger. We already know the result. God wins. The gates of Hades may look pretty dangerous, and they may hurt like hell, but they don't win. That's the gospel.

Meanwhile Peter gets to bind and loose. Many of the controversies in the church today come down to binding and loosing. One bunch of people says the church is doing too much binding and is commanding people to live a certain way when people can't see how they can live that way or why they should. Another bunch of people says the church is doing too much loosing, and it's about time people were told they had to be bound to certain patterns or expectations of life. What both sides need to remember is that the point of binding is to set people free to live disciplined and therefore flourishing lives, while the point of loosing is to bind people more closely to the free Spirit of God. Discipline is for freedom; and freedom is for God.

So this is what the story means for contemporary culture. In a free market of religious choice, in which all the options seem shop soiled, God gives the church the vision to see Jesus, and in Jesus to discover the truth that shapes all other truth. Meanwhile Jesus really did intend the church, and its many failings, individual and corporate, are no surprise to him. The miracle of grace is not just that God wins but that he chooses such fallible creatures as us to be the location of his victory. He trusts his church with mighty responsibilities, and very occasionally it rises to the challenge.

BEFORE THE COCK CROWS

The four gospel accounts of Peter's threefold denial are notable in their similarity and remarkable in their numerous minute differences. Rather than explore each of the four accounts, to keep my treatment succinct, I am going to follow John. This is for two reasons. First, John's version particularly highlights the contrast between Jesus' steadfastness and Peter's faithlessness by placing Peter's first denial before Jesus' interrogation by the high priest and his second and third denials after. Second, considering John's account at this point makes it easier to link Peter's three-fold denial with his later threefold recommissioning, found only in John.

Simon Peter and another disciple were following Jesus. Because this disciple was known to the high priest, he went with Jesus into the high priest's courtyard, but Peter had to wait outside at the door. The other disciple, who was known to the high priest, came back, spoke to the servant girl on duty there and brought Peter in. "You aren't one of this man's disciples too, are you?" she asked Peter. He replied, "I am not." It was cold, and the servants and officials stood around a fire they had made to keep warm. Peter also was standing with them, warming himself.

Meanwhile, the high priest questioned Jesus about his disciples and his teaching. "I have spoken openly to the world," Jesus replied. "I always taught in synagogues or at the temple, where all the Jews come together. I said nothing in secret. Why question me? Ask those who heard me. Surely they know what I said." When Jesus said this, one of the officials nearby slapped him in the face. "Is this the way you answer the high priest?" he demanded. "If I said something wrong," Jesus replied, "testify as to what is wrong. But if I spoke the truth, why did you strike me?" Then Annas sent him bound to Caiaphas the high priest.

Meanwhile, Simon Peter was still standing there warming himself. So they asked him, "You aren't one of his disciples too, are you?" He denied it, saying, "I am not." One of the high priest's servants, a relative of the man whose ear Peter had cut off, challenged him, "Didn't

I see you with him in the garden?" Again Peter denied it, and at that moment a rooster began to crow. (John 18.15–27)

Mark Stibbe very helpfully draws tight connections between this passage and John's earlier description of the sheepfold, which in chapter 2 we discussed in relation to Barabbas. Here are the relevant parts of John 10:

> Very truly I tell you Pharisees, anyone who does not enter the sheep pen by the gate, but climbs in by some other way, is a thief and a robber. The one who enters by the gate is the shepherd of the sheep. The gatekeeper opens the gate for him, and the sheep listen to his voice. He calls his own sheep by name and leads them out.... I am the gate for the sheep. All who have come before me are thieves and robbers, but the sheep have not listened to them.... They will come in and go out, and find pasture. The thief comes only to steal and kill and destroy; I have come that they may have life, and have it to the full.
>
> I am the good shepherd. The good shepherd lays down his life for the sheep. The hired hand is not the shepherd and does not own the sheep. So when he sees the wolf coming, he abandons the sheep and runs away. Then the wolf attacks the flock and scatters it. The man runs away because he is a hired hand and cares nothing for the sheep. I am the good shepherd; I know my sheep and my sheep know me – just as the Father knows me and I know the Father – and I lay down my life for the sheep. (John 10.1–15)

Stibbe points out that the word used for Annas's "courtyard" is the same word as is used in John 10 for "sheepfold". In each passage the "door" is mentioned, again using the identical word. Both passages refer to the gatekeeper, again using the same term. John describes the "other disciple" (often identified with the "Beloved Disciple" who was at Jesus' side at the Last Supper) going into and out of the high priest's house; he uses the same language to talk of the good shepherd going into and out of the sheep pen. Stibbe carefully shows how both the garden of Gethsemane and the high priest's courtyard recall the passage about the Good Shepherd.

> [In the Gethsemane story] the walled garden reminds us of the sheepfold, the approach of Judas reminds us of the thief, the disciples huddled in the garden reminds us of the sheep in the fold, and the protective stance of Jesus reminds us of the good shepherd at the gate.... [In the courtyard of the high priest] the beloved disciple plays the part of the good shepherd who walks in and out of the fold, and the girl at the gate plays the part of the gate-keeper. This leaves Peter, who runs away in the hour of danger.... Peter can only be equated with one role in the shepherd discourse: the role of the hired hand, who runs away in the hour of danger.[4]

And so to the parallel trials. Jesus is surrounded by exalted accusers but stands firm. He stresses that he has spoken the truth (and therefore is open to straightforward contradiction and transparent debate) and that he has spoken openly (and therefore there is no need for furtive questioning, for anyone who had been present could relate what was said). He is in genuine danger of his life. By contrast, Peter is surrounded by shivering servants. There is no suggestion he is in danger of his life: the Beloved Disciple has gone to and fro and the question is simply whether Peter is another such messenger. But Peter evades and denies, becoming an enemy of the truth. Peter has heard Jesus say "I am" many times. Here

Peter says "I am not." Peter has heard Jesus say "I am the light of the world" (John 8.12). Here Peter deprives himself of that light and has to make do with a charcoal fire.

It seems he is there, cold, for quite some time. But he has learned nothing during the wait because he gives exactly the same answer to exactly the same question. The third question has a twist. Peter's enthusiasm, perhaps recklessness, certainly impetuosity, led him to strike off the ear of the high priest's slave at the moment of Jesus' arrest in Gethsemane (John 18.10). This was the disciple who promised so much. Now a relative of that slave is the third to challenge Peter. This is a slightly different denial; Peter has already twice denied the truth of Jesus' teaching by saying he was not among Jesus' disciples; now Peter denies the truth of history by saying he was not with Jesus in the garden. It is not surprising Peter is cold: he has become a shadow of his former self.

This is a harsh version of the lesson that was taught with much more subtlety in the discussion of Nicodemus and Joseph in chapter 3. Peter discovers he cannot have the gospel without Jesus or Jesus without the gospel, and he cannot have either without possible danger. There is no politics without passion. Earlier we discovered in Matthew's account that Peter was a fragile person inspired by God to speak the truth about Jesus. Here in John's account we are reminded just what an extraordinary authority Jesus placed on so fragile a figure. Whatever the politics of the church is founded on, it is clearly not on an authority that never makes mistakes.

ANOTHER CHARCOAL FIRE

When they had finished eating, Jesus said to Simon Peter, "Simon son of John, do you love me more than these?"

"Yes, Lord," he said, "you know that I love you." Jesus said, "Feed my lambs." Again Jesus said, "Simon son of John, do you love me?" He answered, "Yes, Lord, you know that I love you." Jesus said, "Take care of my sheep." The third time he said to him, "Simon son of John, do you love me?" Peter was hurt because Jesus asked him the third time, "Do you love me?" He said, "Lord, you know all things; you know that I love you." Jesus said, "Feed my sheep. Very truly I tell you, when you were younger you dressed yourself and went where you wanted; but when you are old you will stretch out your hands, and someone else will dress you and lead you where you do not want to go." Jesus said this to indicate the kind of death by which Peter would glorify God. Then he said to him, "Follow me!" (John 21.15–19)

Everything in this passage is significant for the way it looks either backward or forward. The setting of the charcoal fire suggests that this is a reprise of Peter's denial in the courtyard of the high priest. The threefold question underlines and confirms the suggestion.

Before going farther, it is worth pausing to recognize the depth of feeling engaged in this story. It is one thing to love another person. It is another for that love to be wrapped around a commitment to learning, following, obeying, and being faithful to a vision, a way of life, a form of human community. It is another again to see the person you love killed and the life you shared destroyed. And it is yet another again to know that you denied that love and that shared life at the very moment when others were agreeing to take that life away. And here is Peter confronted with all of those things, but in a unique form: a man risen from the dead, for whom, it seems, nothing is impossible.

In Matthew's account of the resurrection, Mary Magdalene and the other Mary "hurried away from the tomb, afraid yet filled with joy" (Matt. 28.8). Fear and joy are both profound emotions; together they describe as powerful a feeling as one can imagine. Peter must have felt this acute intersection of feelings on seeing Jesus by the lakeshore. Joy, because the man he loved, and in whose heart he believed lay the destiny of the world, had risen from death and stood before him. Fear, because there was that little matter of his threefold denial. Everyone knows the sinking stomach of the moment when one has to confront the person to whom one has nothing to say but "sorry". But few have as awesome a betrayal to face up to as this.

The whole interchange revolves around two key words: "love" and "know". And to make matters complicated, John uses more than one Greek word for each of them. The exchanges go like this:

agape
filia

> Jesus: Do you love me wholeheartedly and with no thought for yourself, differently from the way you love the others?
>
> Peter: You know that I love you as a friend.
>
> Jesus: Do you love me wholeheartedly and with no thought for yourself?
>
> Peter: You know that I love you as a friend.
>
> Jesus: Do you love me as a friend?
>
> Peter (hurt): You know everything: you realize I love you as a friend.

The conversation can be read on more than one level. It is a discussion, first of all, of whether Jesus can still love Peter, given what he knows. How can you love a person who has let you down badly? Is this foolishness, or forgiveness? It is sometimes said that to understand all is to forgive all – but sometimes the opposite is almost the case. The more Jesus knows about Peter, the hastier his judgements appear, the emptier his promises seem. Peter's folly is not all in the past. Here he is "hurt" that Jesus asks him what sounds like the same question three times. The irony here is poignant; surely it is Jesus, not Peter, who should be hurt. But Peter is still more aware of his own feelings than anyone else's. It is a feature of reconciliation that the person offering forgiveness cannot expect the other party fully to understand the depths of their offence.

On a second level Jesus' repeated question suggests love "knows" in a way impossible without love. Jesus loves Peter – does that make his judgement about Peter better or worse? I recall being told as an undergraduate that I should not study subjects in which I had too great a personal interest – it would cloud my judgement. Similar advice is often given to physicians concerning whom they should treat or to lawyers concerning whom they should represent. And yet does not knowledge belong primarily with love? Have you never heard or seen a news story about someone you knew and cared about and been angry on their behalf because you felt that if the reporter had truly known and cared about the subject of the story they would have presented the facts in a different way? When one imagines God's relationship with every person in creation, it is not just breathtaking that he has created each one; it is even more so that he loves each one and *knows* each one.

On a third level, the conversation begs the question of whether Peter can accept a new relationship with Jesus. A further irony is that Jesus, though betrayed, has not had to reorder his estimation of Peter so much as Peter has had to reshape his understanding of himself. Jesus must always have known Peter's true character, impetuous and flawed as it was (I think this must be the force behind the wording of Peter's third reply); but Peter, it seems, even up to the very day of Jesus' arrest, still thought his own promises of undying loyalty were worth having. He has had to learn a hard lesson. Many people find it very hard indeed to make long-term commitments – in relationships, marriages, working partnerships, or financial endowments. Sometimes this is for fear of being badly hurt – perhaps not for the first time. But sometimes it is through fear of being the one doing the hurting, being the one doing the letting down. Peter has been humiliated to discover he has feet of clay. Being around the resurrected Lord may be an experience of further – perhaps perpetual – humiliation. Well might he keep away.

On a fourth level this conversation exposes what we might call, in the language used throughout this book, the "politics" of friendship. Peter and Jesus simply seem to have different understandings of love. Peter assumes the love of a friend is all that is required. He uses the language of friendship throughout – filial language. It is as if the catastrophe of his betrayal has not taught him that anything was wrong in the love he had for Jesus but only that he had a blip, a fit of absence of mind and heart. He offers to resume that filial love here at the lakeshore. But Jesus is asking for more. Jesus is using the language of utter selfless love, the intimate and self-giving *agape* love that God has for us. In other words, Jesus is saying, "Do you love me as a friend, the way you love everyone else? Or do you love me wholly and utterly, the way I love you?" The pain comes in Peter's reply: "As a friend, of course." And the poignant irony is that Peter doesn't realize what Jesus is asking and thinks he is giving the answer Jesus wants to hear. He even thinks Jesus is being unreasonable in asking the question a third time.

The extraordinary thing is that Jesus entrusts his sheep to Peter even though Peter's love for Jesus is no more than his love for the flock. Jesus doesn't say what we might expect him to say –

"Well, that's not enough, I'm afraid." This passage shows us two significant things about leadership. First, the leader may not necessarily be the best disciple. There is a fantasy inside and outside the church about leaders – that they are people of exceptional vision and courage and that they take their people out of slavery or into the Promised Land by sheer force of personality. But here Peter seems to have less of a relationship with Jesus than Jesus might like, and yet Jesus still entrusts him with the church. How many church leaders feel their relationship with Jesus is less than it might be? And how many might yet find inspiration in their usefulness to God by considering Peter's own shortcomings?

The second, and related, thing we discover about leadership is that every Christian leader is fundamentally first a follower. Time after time Jesus says, "Follow me." Yet nowhere has he said this, in John's gospel, before now. The climax of John's gospel is Jesus saying to Peter, "Follow me." Even after he has been commissioned to shepherd the flock, Peter is called by Jesus to follow. Leaders have no inherent monopoly on what it means to love God – quite the contrary; and they are not exempt from needing to begin again.

FRIENDSHIP AND FORGIVENESS

Although we have been harsh, perhaps a little too harsh, on Peter, we continue to find that each chapter brings us closer to discovering the politics of following Jesus, the intersecting point of power and passion.

Peter's story is a demonstration that passion alone is not enough. Consider his bravado at the Last Supper:

> Then Jesus told them, "This very night you will all fall away on account of me, for it is written: 'I will strike the shepherd, and the sheep of the flock will be scattered.'

But after I have risen, I will go ahead of you into Galilee."
Peter replied, "Even if all fall away on account of you, I
never will." "Truly I tell you," Jesus answered, "this very
night, before the rooster crows, you will disown me three
times." But Peter declared, "Even if I have to die with you,
I will never disown you." (Matt. 26. 31–35)

There is an extraordinary contrast between Peter's blithe
promise of eternal faithfulness ("I will never fall away") and Jesus'
prediction that Peter's fall will be sudden ("this very night, before
the rooster crows"), comprehensive ("you will disown me"), and
impossible to overlook ("three times"). It seems Peter's confidence
is in himself alone; his certainty is in his own conviction.

Peter's passionate promise is a conscious way of exalting himself above all others. When Jesus says "you" to the disciples as a
group, Peter hears "they". He has persuaded himself that he is not
part of that "you" – that he has a special role in salvation that he
cannot lose and that his role seems to rest not on the Lord's com-
mission but on his own qualities of faith and commitment.

Not only does Peter's bravado lead him both to exalt himself
above his friends and to rest his confidence in himself alone; it also
emboldens him to contradict Jesus' very words, not once, but twice.
Jesus says, "You will all fall away"; Peter says, "The others may, but
I shall never." Jesus again says, "Truly you will"; Peter says, "Oh
no, Jesus, I know myself better than you know me – I shall never."
Twice Peter says "never". He speaks of eternity while Jesus speaks
of the present. How can any one of us ever use the word "never"?
How can we assume it applies to us in a way it does not apply to
others? How can we use it when Christ expressly insists "today"?

Three times before in Matthew's gospel, Jesus has reprimanded
Peter for the latter's passionate but wrongheaded commitment.
Each of these occasions exhibits one of the three characteristics

displayed in his bold exchange with Jesus at the Last Supper. We have already seen Peter's words "Never, Lord" when Jesus first predicts his suffering and death in Matthew 16; Peter assumes he knows better than Jesus how salvation is to be attained. Earlier Peter saw Jesus walking on the water and shouted, "Lord, if it's you, tell me to come to you on the water." Jesus called Peter to come to him, and Peter got down out of the boat, walked on the water, and came toward Jesus. But when Peter saw the wind, he became afraid, and, beginning to sink, he cried out, "Lord, save me!" Immediately Jesus reached out his hand and caught him, saying, "You of little faith, why did you doubt?" (Matt. 14.28–31). Here we see Peter's impetuosity, his tendency to speak (and act) first without pausing to consider whether he could sustain his commitment. And later Peter asks Jesus how many times he should forgive someone who sinned against him. He clearly regards seven times as an extraordinary figure. Jesus corrects it with a truly extraordinary figure: seventy times seven (Matt. 18.21–22). Here we see Peter's third uncomfortable characteristic – his tendency to regard his own commitment as exceptional.

Passion alone is not enough. Not just because other things are required but because passionate commitment is often made up of the kinds of tendencies that we see so clearly in Peter – an assumption that one is superior to others, a profound but misplaced confidence in one's own dependability, and a sense that one knows better than Jesus. If passion alone is not enough, what else is needed? I suggest three things.

The first is forgiveness. The forgiveness Jesus brings dissolves the three passionate assumptions Peter makes. It dissolves Peter's arrogance in assuming he had outstanding qualities. Jesus' encounter with Peter by the lakeshore is a commissioning based not on Peter's qualities but on God's grace. As our earlier discussion has demonstrated, Peter does not even love Jesus in a particularly significant way. Peter can never again assume that Jesus has chosen him because he was particularly able or particularly committed or particularly faithful. Peter may never know why Jesus has chosen him. But he will discover that the qualities he will require are ones that only Jesus can provide.

The forgiveness Jesus brings also dissolves Peter's sense of superiority over the other disciples. Peter must know that his denial of Jesus, being set against such grand promises, is as great as any betrayal – save perhaps that of Judas. There is no hope in trying to set himself above his friends – even if he saw any benefit in doing so before. But it is fascinating to see that as soon as Peter is recommissioned by the lakeshore, he is immediately anxious about his status in relation to another disciple. Does Jesus' renewed trust in him make him special, or is there another follower for whom Jesus has a special purpose?

> Peter turned and saw that the disciple whom Jesus loved was following them. (This was the one who had leaned back against Jesus at the supper and had said, "Lord, who is going to betray you?") When Peter saw him, he asked, "Lord, what about him?" Jesus answered, "If I want him to remain alive until I return, what is that to you? You must follow me." (John 21.20–22)

Peter cannot leave it alone. He somehow struggles to realize that Jesus' forgiveness means a restoration to wholehearted love. Peter is still anxious that the role of the so-called Beloved Disciple will somehow get in the way. "But what about him?" He finds it hard to see how Jesus is free of the small-mindedness of human regard. Jesus bluntly reiterates that this is not Peter's problem: "What is that to you?" And then he simply repeats the simple call to Peter to renew his discipleship in response to the new life he has been offered through resurrection and forgiveness: "Follow me."

Jesus' forgiveness dissolves Peter's third tendency – his habit of assuming he knows better than Jesus. We have already observed the intensity of his exchange in response to the question, "Do you love me?" Peter still cannot quite realize that Jesus' logic is unassailable. Jesus' logic is the logic of resurrection – a logic unique to Jesus, without comparison, analogy, or alternative. Much as it is understandable that Peter struggles with this new logic, it is not commendable. For Christians, the logic of forgiveness is not essentially a logic that says that everyone deserves a second chance, that bitterness hurts the victim more than the sinner, or that time heals most things. The logic of forgiveness has no foundation other than resurrection. Resurrection knows the power of death yet loves with the force of life. This is the only logic that truly sustains forgiveness.

Forgiveness is therefore vital to any politics that goes beyond passion. And similarly essential is friendship. Friendship disciplines passion in a number of significant ways, as Peter discovers. Friendship earths noble ideals. It would be hard for anyone to know whether Peter still felt inspired by salvation, truth, and justice; such abstract nouns are hard to measure – or to oppose. But each of the gospel writers describes vividly how Peter denied his true friend Jesus, and somehow any aspiration to noble ideals seems to count for little in relation to this rejection. It is often said that soldiers in battle are much more likely to give their lives for their comrades in arms than for any noble ideals for which the battle is supposedly being fought. Many would share the hope that if they had to choose between their friends and their country, they would choose their friends (although the view was considered scandalous when enunciated by the novelist E. M. Forster in the 1930s). Peter learns that his following Jesus has brought him a whole new set of friends; when following Jesus becomes difficult, his loyalty to those friends should save him, even if his faith in Jesus fails him.

Friendship deserves respect only if it has survived bad weather as well as good. Associations developed in happy times need to be tested in hard times if they are truly to be regarded as friendships. Most of us know how the sheep scatter in the face of illness, the loss of face, or the ending of a relationship. But it is almost equally the case that associations formed in sad and needy times must be allowed to expand to incorporate the carefree moments of happiness if they are not to become prisons. It is a commonplace that one spends three years at university trying to lose the friends one made in the first week. Likewise a friend made in the intensity of a twelve-step program may not always be a person who allows one to spread one's wings and fly again after learning to live with addiction. Peter's friendship with Jesus knew wonderful times – one can only imagine the joy of a miraculous catch of fish, literally and metaphorically, the wonder of healing, and the awe of transfiguration. But it had also known hard times – the storm at sea and the rising tide of opposition from the Jerusalem authorities. It was a true friendship, which is what made its betrayal so agonizing.

And one further dimension of friendship disclosed by the scene at the lakeside is that friendship involves food. The meaning of *companion* is a person with whom one shares bread. At the Last Supper, when Peter declares his eternal loyalty, Jesus breaks bread and pours wine. At the lakeshore, when Jesus restores Peter to mission, discipleship, and friendship, Jesus again takes the bread. Bread is mentioned specifically in this story, even though it seems to be a story about fish. Hence this is a story about Jesus' not just forgiving Peter but once again becoming his friend – his companion, his bread-sharer. The test of whether their forgiveness is real is whether they can sit down and share a meal together. This is why the Eucharist is so central to the life of the church: it is the moment when God's people sit down and eat with him and with one another, with those who need to forgive them and those they need to forgive.

So beyond passion lies forgiveness and friendship. And what this means is the beginning of a new understanding of power. The first four chapters of this book have each portrayed characters who had a certain degree of power. Pilate saw power as acquiring a monopoly over the key elements of social control such as patronage and taxation and underwriting his diplomacy with the constant threat of military coercion. Barabbas largely shared Pilate's notion of power and believed that power should be transferred to those who trace their heritage to King David. Barabbas knew the power of strict discipline of body and spirit in building a subversive force, but in the end he assumed real change could come only through violent insurrection. The Jewish authorities, in different ways, accepted Pilate's definition of power. They were attracted by the wealth, prestige, and security that allegiance to Rome could offer. The nadir of their political outlook comes in their words in John's passion account: "We have no king but Caesar" (John 19.15). Even those who were very much inclined toward Jesus, Nicodemus and Joseph of Arimathea, had no ability to see beyond the cross; their politics was mesmerized by Roman power. In Mrs Pilate we began to see a slightly different notion of power. We saw the power of sexual jealousy, the power of dreams, and the power of personal magnetism. Whether we see Mrs Pilate as powerful or powerless in Roman terms, we see in her that power and politics are not just about coercion, wealth, and public office.

In this chapter we have begun to see some of the key components of the politics of Jesus. We have seen starkly what they do not require – outstanding gifts, a sense of superiority over others, unquestioning confidence in the correctness of one's own opinions. Peter had all of these, but none were helpful to his discipleship – in fact, quite the opposite. Peter struggled to see the two foundations of Jesus' version of power. The first is the acceptance of the cross. Peter was horrified when the idea is first announced in Matthew 16, and even in the garden of Gethsemane, when the crucifixion had become almost inevitable, Peter still took up a sword and lopped off the ear of the high priest's servant (John 18.10). The second foundation is the transformation of resurrection. Peter struggled with the details (the strips of linen and the cloths that had been wrapped around Jesus' head), whereas the Beloved Disciple "saw and believed" (John 20.8). But Jesus had a special resurrection appearance in store for Peter. And that appearance by the lakeshore, as we have seen, shows that resurrection is intimately related to forgiveness and friendship.

Resurrection is tied to friendship because otherwise, as we saw earlier with passion, it could quickly become abstract. Who could be against resurrection, after all? But tied to friendship, resurrection becomes a matter of the transformation of real people, known and loved over time, in sorrow and in joy, and emerging by God's power from the prison of death. What power could be greater than this? If death is no longer to be feared, what can Rome, what can any coercive power, do to intimidate and oppress? And when resurrection is tied to forgiveness, it addresses the worst horrors left unresolved in human experience. If Peter can find a place once again in Jesus' heart, we all can. If Jesus has a significant role for Peter to play, impetuous and unreliable as Peter is, then he has a role for each one of us. The most powerful force in human experience, the heart of politics, is not, it seems, the might of Rome and the merciless will of the governor; it is Jesus' cross and resurrection and the friendship and forgiveness they make possible.

OPPORTUNITIES FOR INDIVIDUAL
OR GROUP REFLECTION

I wonder whether the people Jesus founds the church on today are as fragile as Peter.

I wonder what it feels like to find out that a church leader has feet of clay.

I wonder what it is like to play in a game when one already knows the result.

I wonder how one comes to suppose one knows better than Jesus.

I wonder what it is like to feel that the other disciples are not as committed as you.

I wonder what it is like to realize you have made a promise you cannot keep.

I wonder what it is like to know you have let down the most important person in the world.

I wonder what it is like to know that everyone knows you have let them down.

I wonder what it is like to see again someone you have hurt very badly indeed.

I wonder what it feels like to be given another chance.

✓ I wonder what it is like to feel you cannot love as much as you are loved.

✓ I wonder what it is like to become friends again.

✓ I wonder whether it is possible to know someone has left you on the point of death – and still to love them.

Lord God of mercy and forgiveness,
whose Son, Jesus Christ, was so sorely betrayed
yet was so quick to restore his disciples to trust and
    authority:
we confess before you that we your church
have often been stupid, selfish, scared, and just plain wrong;
we have sat around a charcoal fire
and let our faithfulness to you unravel
in the face of expediency, shortsightedness, and fear.

Yet you have met us at another charcoal fire:
you have loved us even though you know us,
and you have shown us the possibilities of friendship
and the politics of limitless love.

Make us so overwhelmed at the enormity of your
    commission to us,
so overjoyed at your trust in us,
and so overawed at the love you have for us,
that we answer your call with faith, repay your trust with
    hope,
and show forth your love in resurrection glory. Amen.

CHAPTER 6

MARY MAGDALENE

We come to the final character of our six Passiontide witnesses. In this chapter we discover how power and passion come together in unexpected ways. We find where the politics of Jesus really lies.

Mary Magdalene is a figure who has attracted endless fascination. There seem to be so many Marys in the Gospels – the mother of Jesus, the sister of Martha and Lazarus, the wife of Clopas, the mother of James and Joseph – that it is understandable that readers have been inclined to conflate these various characters. References to there having been seven demons cast out of her (Luke 8.2) and to "a woman in that town who lived a sinful life" (Luke 7.37) have tended to be combined to shape Mary Magdalene as a character of strong emotions and a colorful past. The treatment in this chapter does not enter into scholarly and popular speculation and imagination to any degree. It simply looks at three specific references to Mary Magdalene's presence at significant moments in the account of Jesus' death and resurrection and prefaces the discussion with a consideration of the story of the anointing at Bethany – a story in which the woman is not named but whose actions are in character with the Mary Magdalene we shall go on to encounter.

THE TRANSFORMATION OF PASSION

Now the Passover and the Festival of Unleavened Bread were only two days away, and the chief priests and the teachers of the law were looking for some sly way to arrest Jesus and kill him. "But not during the Festival," they said, "or the people may riot." While he was in Bethany, reclining at the table in the home of Simon the Leper, a woman came with an alabaster jar of very expensive perfume, made of pure nard. She broke the jar and poured the perfume on his head. Some of those present were saying indignantly to one another, "Why this waste of perfume? It could have been sold for more than a year's wages and the money given to the poor." And they rebuked her harshly. "Leave her alone," said Jesus. "Why are you bothering her? She has done a beautiful thing to me. The poor you will always have with you, and you can help them any time you want. But you will not always have me. She did what she could. She poured perfume on my body beforehand to prepare for my burial. Truly I tell you, wherever the gospel is preached throughout the world, what she has done will also be told, in memory of her." Then Judas Iscariot, one of the Twelve, went to the chief priests to betray Jesus to them. They were delighted to hear this and promised to give him money. So he watched for an opportunity to hand him over. (Mark 14.1 – 11)

This is the beginning of Mark's account of Jesus' passion. It unites the twin themes of passion as voluntary suffering and passion as overwhelming love. The woman in the story is commended so highly because she is like Jesus – she faces the disapproval of the community (and therefore suffers) in order to demonstrate her overwhelming love. In the process she gives us a little picture of God's love for us in Jesus – a love which is overwhelming, is poured out over us, and results in Jesus' suffering. Alone of all the disciples, this woman fully appreciates that Jesus is facing death.

This passage has important things to say about the when, where, how, and who of the passion and power of Jesus. We shall look at each of these in turn.

The *when* of the passion and power of Jesus is found in the three references to time in this story. First, this event takes place when "the Passover and the Festival of Unleavened Bread were only two days away". The Passover was the great feast celebrating the way the Lord had liberated his people from slavery in Egypt, remembering the hasty meal they had eaten before their journey and the blood of the lamb they had painted on their doorposts so the angel of the Lord would not strike them down as he did the Egyptians. So the politics of this woman comes in the context of God setting people free. The gospel is always about God setting his people free to be his friends again.

The second reference to time refers to the event at which Jesus is present. It is dinner at the house of Simon the Leper. The passion and power of Jesus are particularly made visible in the sharing of food. The Eucharist, or Holy Communion, is many things – a remembrance and reenactment of the Last Supper and a foretaste of the heavenly banquet, to name the two most obvious. But it is at heart a meal shared with God at which Jesus is present and at which the guests expect transformation to take place. That is what happens in this story. That is what one should expect every time God's people gather to eat a meal with Jesus. For Jesus is God setting his people free to be his friends again.

The third reference to time refers to a time without Jesus. "You will not always have me." The time spent with Jesus is time in which disciples must learn how to spend time without Jesus.

The woman in this story realizes that Jesus has not come among his people to remind them of truths they already knew. Jesus does not simply confirm the deductions of common sense or the wisest estimations of widespread reflection. He brings a new reality and requires acts of courage and sacrifice that make no sense without him. The woman's action is absurd outside a context in which it mirrors and anticipates the absurdity of the love of God. But within that context, it makes perfect sense. Every time a disciple makes a gesture that attracts widespread criticism because it goes against what everybody thinks or knows and yet is congruent with the whole direction of Jesus' ministry, people will recall this story about a woman who did the same herself.

Moving to the *where* of this story, again three features are significant. First, the incident takes place in Bethany, which is only a few miles from Jerusalem, where "the chief priests and the teachers of the law were looking for some sly way to arrest Jesus and kill him." In other words, the politics of following Jesus assumes a context of danger. The whole conversation and the events surrounding it are beside a snake pit; one wrong move and Jesus will be attacked and fatally bitten.

Next, Jesus' companions at dinner are a hostile bunch. The politics of following Jesus assumes a context of controversy in which gestures will be made, misunderstood, criticized, attacked and in which every action will be commented upon and need to be explained, justified, supported, defended. It must have been exhausting following Jesus. Not only was he constantly on the move and constantly making greater demands of his disciples, but he was also endlessly caught in controversy, relentlessly in dialogue with those who were out to undermine, misrepresent, and discredit his ministry. Controversy is not in itself a sign that one's discipleship is faithful, but if no one is out to undermine you, after a time you must begin to wonder whether you have left

Bethany for quieter surroundings. "Woe to you when everyone speaks well of you, for that is how their ancestors treated the false prophets" (Luke 6.26).

And the third issue of location in this story is that it takes place in the house of a leper. In modern medicine, leprosy refers to one specific disease caused by one specific bug that causes skin sores and destroys nerves, meaning that patients lose their fingers and toes due to repeated injury from lack of feeling. For the gospel writers, leprosy refers to a variety of skin diseases, some more infectious than others. What they all had in common was that they made the sufferer unclean. Ironically, Jesus' companions at dinner object to the treatment he receives from the woman but seem not to be troubled by his eating with a man who is ritually unclean. The house of a person with a notorious and unsightly disease completes the significant contexts of this story. Jesus is in a place of danger, of controversy, of social exclusion, and of chronic sickness. These are typical environments for his passion and politics.

Now we move to the *how* of Jesus' politics. At each stage we are getting closer and closer to the heart of who Jesus is and how his transformation comes. Again we shall look at three dimensions of what it means to engage in the power and passion of Jesus. First we are aware that this is a story about intimate touch of the body. No one can be in any doubt that intimate touch of the body is about both passion and power. The character Mary Magdalene in the musical drama *Jesus Christ Superstar* famously sings, "I don't know how to love him – what to do, how he moves me." People in the church are terrified of talking about the intimate touch of the body, both because of the litany of cases in which vulnerable people, especially children, have been manipulated and seriously harmed, and also because of an abiding sense of danger and disclosure about the electricity of intimate touch. But in this story the woman's touch has several features that may inspire us to value such touch while being careful and conscious of its misuse. Her touch is public: there is no suggestion of anything furtive or behind closed doors. It is ritualized: she is clearly following the procedures associated with burial rites. It is limited: she touches only Jesus' head. It is done by a vulnerable woman to a powerful man: thus it reverses the conventional cycle of dubious gratification and the misappropriation of authority. And it happens only once.

What we see here is a complement to what we saw in the previous chapter. Peter's shortcoming was that he mistook his own passion for Jesus' power. Here we see that the woman's passion is a suitable analogy for Jesus' power. There can be no politics without passion. But passion can never simply be passion-as-overwhelming-love; it must always also be passion-as-voluntary-suffering.

It is almost taken for granted in some circles that all intimate touch is some kind of more or less sublimated sexual impulse. It is as if we are all Freudians now. But could it not be the case that all intimate touch, including but by no means limited to tender sexual touch, is a search for the gentle touch of God? The parent carefully changing the soiled clothes of a baby, the caregiver deftly assisting a frail, elderly person into the bath, the friend offering a handkerchief and perhaps a sheltering arm to comfort the neighbor in grief or despair: these are all occasions of gentle touch and intimations of the gesture of the woman in Simon's house – but they can hardly be called erotic. The politics of Jesus' power and passion is shaped by intimate gestures like these.

A further dimension of the *how* disclosed in this passage is the woman's extravagance. The perfume was worth a year's wages. Think of all the useful things that could have been done with such a sum of money. There is a profound irony here. However useful these projects might have been, it is fairly certain that none of them would have inspired and moved countless millions of people hundreds – and now thousands – of years later. To be part of the way God transforms the lives of his people through the centuries – a year's wages seems pretty cheap for such a prize. History proved the woman right.

But there is still a nagging anxiety that the criticism is right – that waste is wrong in principle, and the waste of transferable wealth that could benefit the disadvantaged is invariably wrong in practice. Such a view deep down assumes that the fundamental problem with the world is the shortage of resources and that the fundamental solution is an incremental redistribution of those resources. Simply to pour resources away – to empty a jar of pure nard – is thus a terrible thing. But this view, though widely held, does not seem to be Jesus' view. Jesus does not live in a world of scarcity. For him, the defining force is the love of his Father, of which there is more than enough for everybody and plenty besides. For Jesus, the glorious abundance of the woman's perfume epitomizes the extravagant gesture of God's love in sending his own Son. Both are far too much for the world's imagination. The world does indeed have a problem, but the problem is not so much scarcity as it is sin. Scarcity was created by sin. Because of sin, however well resourced the world might be, some would still be disadvantaged, because sharing is never popular, whether among two-year-olds at a nursery or among cartels forming a monopoly. Jesus points back at his critical dinner companions and says, "By simply giving money to the poor, you are confirming social relations as they stand – just alleviating the pressure a little. This woman understands that what is needed is transformation of self and society, a transformation that changes the location of power through dismantling the stranglehold of death and makes this woman's kind of passion central because it points to the new kind of power. She realizes that that is the transformation I am about to bring about."

The third dimension of the way the woman demonstrates the power and passion of Jesus is that she understands beauty. There is an overwhelming contrast between the calculations of those who assess the monetary value of the perfume, those who miss the significance of the gesture because they are speculating and murmuring and plotting, and the simple beauty of the gesture itself. "She has done a beautiful thing to me", says Jesus. The woman has captured the wordless energy of grief. there is nothing to say, no way to make things better, no way to bring happiness into the situation, but that does not mean there is nothing that can be done. Think of scenes of great local and national tragedy in recent years; think of the countless bunches of flowers that appear at roadsides or at civic or church buildings as small and beautiful tokens of grief. Of course it is a waste of money, but the sight of a mass of flowers is sometimes a more lasting memory than a host of useful interventions. It is a beautiful thing.

In the town where I live there are around thirty-five murders a year, mostly from gunshots. A group of people has taken to gathering at the site of each murder to keep a silent vigil for the death that has taken place and to offer prayers. The purpose of these prayer vigils is to bring people together to honor the lives of the victims, to comfort the family, friends, and neighbors, to pray for peace and healing in the neighborhood and throughout the town, to allow those affected the opportunity to have their voices heard and their grief acknowledged, and to protest publicly to the community the conviction that such violence is unacceptable and requires all those who want to promote justice and mercy to take action. These vigils are occasions of great beauty in just the way that the gesture of the woman in Bethany was an event of great beauty. They are sometimes welcomed, sometimes misunderstood. But they are in a good tradition of humble gestures that point to the gesture of Christ. Sometimes one cannot make things happy, but one can still make things beautiful.

And last we turn to the *who* of the passion and power of Jesus as disclosed by this story. Again there are three points to make. The first is that Jesus' power and passion are intimately intertwined with the poor. There is only one way to make sense of his words, "The poor you will always have with you", and that is, "You will always be with the poor." There are all sorts of ways to avoid the poor – to live in a neighborhood where one neither mixes with (day by day) nor even passes by (on the way to work or school) anyone whose social difference feels uncomfortable to either party. Another is to retreat into ideology, to convince oneself and seek to convince others that the poor are poor only because they are lazy or foolish or crooked and that no positive action can change the situation – and to block out any personal relationship or local initiative that suggests otherwise. Another is to place all one's energy in finding and funding solutions on a strategic and "macro" level. Each of these is a different way of avoiding personal encounter, any possible friendship that might mean "the poor are always with you". It is hard to bring about real change in other people's lives and circumstances if one is not open to real change in one's own. The relationship that brings about real change is friendship. There is no evidence that Jesus' critical companions at Bethany had any intention of building real relationships with the people they describe as "the poor". The poor were just a stick with which to beat Jesus.

The heart of Jesus' engagement with the poor is not so much that he worked *for* them by changing their situation for the better (although sometimes he did) nor so much that he worked *with* them by assisting their methods of improving their own circumstances; it was that he *was* with the poor in such a way that the poor were never a "they" but always an "us". Jesus' response to poverty was incarnation. He was thirty years in Nazareth being with the oppressed people of God before he ever set off for Jerusalem to make a fundamental change possible. He was born in a stable, had no place to lay his head, died among criminals; he was always with the poor. This was his politics and his passion.

The story of the anointing at Bethany offers us another insight into the identity of passionate discipleship: it is anonymous. We do not know the name of the woman who made this extravagant gesture. I have treated her under the heading of Mary Magdalene because her gesture is true to the character I shall shortly describe, but Mark does not reveal her identity. She deserves the description given by George Eliot for the central character Dorothea in the closing words of her novel *Middlemarch*:

> For there is no creature whose inward being is so strong that it is not greatly determined by what lies outside it. A new Theresa will hardly have the opportunity of reforming a conventional life, any more than a new Antigone will spend her heroic piety in daring all for the sake of a brother's burial: the medium in which their ardent deeds took shape is for ever gone. But we insignificant people with our daily words and acts are preparing the lives of many Dorotheas, some of which may present a far sadder sacrifice than that of the Dorothea whose story we know.
>
> Her finely touched spirit had still its fine issues, though they were not widely visible. Her full nature, like that river of which Cyrus broke the strength, spent itself in channels which had no great name on the earth. But the effect of her being on those around her was incalculably diffusive: for the growing good of the world is partly dependent on unhistoric acts; and that things are not so

ill with you and me as they might have been, is half owing to the number who lived faithfully a hidden life, and rest in unvisited tombs.

The woman at the center of the anointing story certainly rests in an unvisited tomb. She is content that any story that may involve her is remembered as a story that is really about Jesus. It is often said that there is no limit to what can be achieved so long as one does not mind who gets the credit. The politics of passionate discipleship is powerful because – and when – it has said goodbye to the cultivation of reputation or the acclamation of posterity.

And the last thing that must be said about this story is that the one who sees what no one else can see, and loves as no one else loves, and does what no one else does, is a woman. As we are about to see, Mark's gospel is a story in which the male disciples fade away through stupidity, sin, and shame. Only this woman anticipates Jesus' burial; only women disciples witness his burial. "Whoever wants to become great among you must be your servant" (Mark 10.43), says Jesus, and no one epitomizes this more than the woman at Bethany. She above all shows the centrality of passion to the emerging new notion of power. She, and others like her, must be the center of the new politics.

THE TRANSFORMATION OF TRAGEDY

We have established the contours of the passion of Jesus' politics. We now pause to see how this passion withstands suffering and death before considering further the heart of where the power of Jesus' politics lies.

For Matthew and Mark, Mary Magdalene and Mary the mother of James and Joseph are unique. They alone witness Jesus' death, observe Jesus' burial, and discover the empty tomb.

The curtain of the temple was torn in two from top to bottom. And when the centurion, who stood there in front of Jesus, saw how he died, he said, "Surely this man was the Son of God!" Some women were watching from a distance. Among them were Mary Magdalene, Mary the mother of James the younger and of Joseph, and Salome. In Galilee these women had followed him and cared for his needs. Many other women who had come up with him to Jerusalem were also there....

So Joseph bought some linen cloth, took down the body, wrapped it in the linen, and placed it in a tomb cut out of rock. Then he rolled a stone against the entrance of the tomb. Mary Magdalene and Mary the mother of Joseph saw where he was laid.

When the Sabbath was over, Mary Magdalene, Mary the mother of James, and Salome bought spices so that they might go to anoint Jesus' body. Very early on the first day of the week, just after sunrise, they were on their way to the tomb and they asked each other, "Who will roll the stone away from the entrance of the tomb?" (Mark 15.38–41; 15.46–16.3)

Here are three episodes that continue some of the themes highlighted in the anointing at Bethany. Most obviously, it is women who dominate the story at its lowest ebb. The male disciples, at least the original ones, are nowhere to be seen; only Joseph appears from the shadows, and he is an ambivalent character, as we have discovered. (John's gospel has the Beloved Disciple with Jesus' mother at the foot of the cross, but the Beloved Disciple is in every way an exceptional follower.) Just as at Bethany the woman alone was able to perceive the inevitability of Jesus' coming death, likewise now at the cross the women alone are able to face the reality of the cross. One would have thought that the debate in the following centuries would not have been on the question of whether women could lead God's people but about whether men could.

And what is it precisely that the women in this account do that the men it seems cannot? The summary at the end of the crucifixion scene mentions three things. They follow Jesus. This has been the simple call throughout the gospel narrative. The disciples have heard it, responded to it, shared it with others, and been rewarded with Jesus' intimate teaching and his careful prediction of what lay ahead – and then those disciples have scattered. At a distance, following humbly, with no fanfare, no false promises, no drama, are the women. What a wonderful epitaph: "She followed." Only one man seems to follow Jesus in such an uncomplicated way in Mark's gospel, and that is Bartimaeus. In Mark 10.52 we read, " 'Go,' said Jesus, 'your faith has healed you.' Immediately he received his sight and followed Jesus along the road." But even Bartimaeus is elsewhere at the cross.

The women's faithful following meant a second thing: they "cared for his needs". No action fulfils this description better than going to the tomb with spices when the Sabbath was over. As Mark's gospel has progressed, discipleship has come to emerge as this straightforward pattern of service, epitomized by the table-waiter, or deacon. The climax of this description is these words of Jesus:

> You know that those who are regarded as rulers of the Gentiles lord it over them, and their high officials exercise authority over them. Not so with you. Instead, whoever wants to become great among you must be your servant, and whoever wants to be first must be slave of all. For even the Son of Man did not come to be served, but

to serve, and to give his life as a ransom for many. (Mark 10.42–45)

Ched Myers comments on this passage – and the disparity between male and female disciples – giving four possible interpretations.

[It could be] a polemic against the actual Jerusalem-based church led by Peter, James, John, and Jesus' own family members, a position I think over speculative. Another option is that Mark simply wished to discredit any and all forms of leadership per se. This interpretation, too, I think is forced, for Mark does not dismiss but redefines the vocation of leadership; "leaderless groups" are, I think, a fantasy of modernism. More credible is a third possibility, that the story was meant to encourage critical accountability by those who "assume" leadership in the community. The negative portrait of the male disciples would certainly have ... reminded the whole community that leaders can and do fail, and exhorted all to guard against the inevitable delusions of power that accrue in any social group. I think the narrative does encourage this, but this is not its primary function.

The fourth possibility is that in a thoroughly patriarchal socio-cultural order, women alone are fit to act as servant-leaders.... How else can a portrait that paints men as power-hungry and women as servants function, except to legitimate women as leaders?[5]

The third dimension that underlines the previous two lies in the little phrase "other women who had come up with him to Jerusalem". Why "up"? Prepositions are often very telling. For example, it is common for British people to talk of friends being "out in Zambia" or "out in Nepal", but they would never say "out in New York". The word "out" somehow denotes something exotic or demanding. This little word "up" in this context in Mark has a similar force. It points to the way that going to Jerusalem is the climax of Jesus' ministry. It underlines the fact that these women appreciated the importance of Jesus' journey on the way of the cross. This feature, the perseverance of the women, continues in the description of Jesus' burial. For those who have attended painful funerals with few present to give grief some (at least temporary) wider social significance, the account of Jesus' being buried with a congregation of two may offer some consolation. Mary Magdalene and the other Mary saw where he was laid. They were witnesses.

In my discussion of the anointing at Bethany, I drew out what I described as the passionate politics of the unnamed woman. In my account of Peter's passion in the previous chapter, I suggested that its weakness was precisely that it lacked power – that it evaporated when the heat was turned up. But Mary Magdalene's passion, as we have seen in this treatment of the death and burial of Jesus, is made of sterner stuff than Peter's. What gives Mary Magdalene's passion a genuine politics, a sustainable way of engaging with the world over a lifetime, with a strength that Peter's lacks? The answer is that Mary Magdalene's passion is genuinely Christ's passion, with a power that is rooted in resurrection, as we shall now see.

THE TRANSFORMATION OF POWER

The woman of passion, who had been faithful to the very end, the woman whose actions are summed up in the extravagant pouring out of costly perfume over the head of the Lord in love and service and recognition of proximity to death, now discovers the power that transforms the politics of the world.

> Early on the first day of the week, while it was still dark, Mary Magdalene went to the tomb and saw that the stone had been removed from the entrance. So she came running to Simon Peter and the other disciple, the one Jesus loved, and said, "They have taken the Lord out of the tomb, and we don't know where they have put him!" ...
>
> Now Mary stood outside the tomb crying. As she wept, she bent over to look into the tomb and saw two angels in white, seated where Jesus' body had been, one at the head and the other at the foot. They asked her, "Woman, why are you crying?" "They have taken my Lord away," she said, "and I don't know where they have put him." At this, she turned around and saw Jesus standing there, but she did not realize that it was Jesus. He asked her, "Woman, why are you crying? Who is it you are looking for?" Thinking he was the gardener, she said, "Sir, if you have carried him away, tell me where you have put him, and I will get him." Jesus said to her, "Mary." She turned toward him and cried out in Aramaic, "Rabboni!" (which means "Teacher"). Jesus said, "Do not hold on to me, for I have not yet ascended to the Father. Go instead to my brothers and tell them, 'I am ascending to my Father and your Father, to my God and your God.'" Mary Magdalene went to the disciples with the news: "I have seen the Lord!" And she told them that he had said these things to her. (John 20.1–2, 11–18)

I shall read this story three times – once in relation to what is revealed by the way the story is structured, a second time in relation to where this passage stands in the whole story of the Bible, and a third time in relation to the issues of power and passion discussed in this book.

Beginning with the way the story is structured, we may follow the analysis of Mark Stibbe, who suggests that verses 11–18 form four closely related segments.[6] The account begins with Mary Magdalene speaking with two angels. It concludes with her announcing the good news to the disciples. When one realizes that the Greek for *angels* (*angelloi*) is almost identical to the Greek for *announce* (*angello*), it becomes apparent that these words give a symmetry to the opening and closing of the scene. That isolates the two conversations in between. These two conversations, the first with the angels and the second with Jesus, have a parallel shape. Each begins with the identical words, "Woman, why are you crying?" (The second conversation adds the phrase "Who is it you are looking for?" – a phrase that Jesus twice asks to those who came to arrest him in Gethsemane and a question at the very heart of the gospel.) Then each conversation continues with a lament from Mary Magdalene, seeking the location of Jesus' body and repeating her words to Peter and the Beloved Disciple at the start of the chapter. And in each case Mary then turns – the first time to see Jesus, but not to recognize him (like most of the people in the gospel story), the second time to see and believe. So the structure is as follows:

1. Mary Magdalene meets the "announcers".
2. Mary Magdalene is questioned, laments, and turns.
3. Mary Magdalene is questioned again (almost identically), laments again (almost identically), and turns again (very differently).
4. Mary Magdalene becomes an "announcer".

Moving to the place of this passage in the whole story of the Bible, I want now to suggest that each of these four segments of the encounter between Mary Magdalene and the risen Lord has a significant relationship with an overarching theme in the whole sweep of Scripture. Let me begin with the simplest of the four themes. This is the first day of the week, and this is a man and a woman in a garden. There could hardly be three more explicit references to the creation story in Genesis. John is offering us a new Adam and Eve, putting right the fatal error of the fall and describing the nature of the new creation. This is quite simply a new creation story. It is as grand as that. Humanity fell again in Gethsemane when the disciples scattered and hid, just as it had fallen in Eden, when the man and the woman hid. But here it is, three days later, restored, redeemed, transformed. Mary mistook Jesus for the gardener. How stupid she seems – until we realize that Jesus *is* the gardener, Jesus is the Word who was with the Father when God made the garden – the whole of creation, epitomized by Eden. This is the great theme of what I have called segment 2.

And the great theme picked up by the third segment is that of God's longing search for his people. One of the most neglected books in the Bible is the Song of Songs, a collection of love poems with some explicit references to physical love that have perhaps brought about its exclusion from the conventional Sunday School curriculum. Here we read:

> All night long on my bed I looked for the one my heart loves; I looked for him but did not find him. I will get up now and go about the city, through its streets and squares; I will search for the one my heart loves. So I looked for him but did not find him. The watchmen found me as they made their rounds in the city. "Have you seen the one my heart loves?" Scarcely had I passed them when I found the one my heart loves. I held him and would not let him go. (Song of Songs 3.1–4)

Song of Songs makes sense when we read in it the aching desire God has for his people. Mary Magdalene, like the woman who anointed Jesus at Bethany, imitates the love of God by the way she achingly searches for Jesus. And of course when she finds him she clings to him – just as in the poem the woman says, "I held him and would not let him go." The Old Testament is a love story, in which God and Israel dance and promise and separate and reconcile. And Jesus makes plain that he has come finally to win Israel's heart forever. If Mary Magdalene imitates God in this passage, she also represents Israel, hesitantly at first but finally turning to embrace the love of God in Christ. There is joy among the angels.

The great theme picked up by segment 1 emerges when one wonders why John has given us one of his characteristic details – in the phrase "two angels in white, seated where Jesus' body had been, *one at the head and the other at the foot*" (20.12). There is another very important place where angels sit at either end of a structure roughly the same size as Jesus' burial plinth. Consider this passage from Exodus 25.17–22, where God tells Moses how he will be encountered by the Israelites – how his covenant will be embodied:

> Make an atonement cover of pure gold – two and a half cubits long and a cubit and a half wide. And make *two cherubim out of hammered gold at the ends of the cover.* Make *one cherub on one end and the second cherub on the other*; make the cherubim of one piece with the cover, at the two ends. The cherubim are to have their wings spread upward, overshadowing the cover with them. The cherubim are to face each other, looking toward the cover. Place the cover on top of the ark and put in the ark the tablets of the covenant law that I will give you. *There, above the cover between the two cherubim* that are over the ark of

the covenant law, *I will meet with you* and give you all my commands for the Israelites. (my italics)

This is the only encounter with angels in the whole of John's gospel. They appear in order to echo the cherubim on either end of the ark of the covenant. They announce that the new place of encounter of God and his people is not the tablets of the Ten Commandments in a sealed box (a box lost in the exile 500 years before Christ) but is instead the power of the risen Jesus, meeting people in despair.

And so the great theme that emerges explicitly in segment 4 is, quite simply, the gospel – the good news whose spread is the subject of the rest of the New Testament, particularly the Acts of the Apostles, beginning with Mary Magdalene's words to the disciples, "I have seen the Lord!"

And these four dimensions of John's account express what we might call the politics of resurrection. The *power* of Jesus' resurrection is the power of creation – new creation. Jesus is alive, not just in the same way as he raised Lazarus to life but in a new way – Jesus will never die again. The power of death is broken. The boundaries of possibility are crossed. No longer is it the grave that holds the unknowns; all wonder, all worship turns to God, to Jesus the bringer of life. When Mary turns, she turns from darkness to light, from despair to hope, from death to life. This is the unparalleled power of resurrection. Not only is the future open; the past is transformed. The possibility of forgiveness, as we saw in the last chapter in relation to Peter, means that one can begin to reclaim the past as a friend rather than as an enemy. Life does not need to be lived running away from regrets or running away from death. This is true freedom – and a new power.

The *passion* of Jesus' resurrection lies in its fulfilling the aching search of God for his people. In the encounter between the new man and the renewed woman in the garden on the first day of the week we see a picture of the passionate love of God for us, and the longing, desire, and joy that overcome both parties in their reconciliation and new covenant. Resurrection is the vindication of the passion of Mary Magdalene, the passion of persistent faithfulness at cross and tomb, and resurrection is the announcement that the overwhelming love of God is not to be withstood forever. Passion is no longer tragic, a doleful, melancholic love for the lost. Passion is now an advance token of final fulfillment – a longing for union that may be experienced now as suffering but will in due course be consummated in union with God.

In its evocation of the ark of the covenant, the resurrection of Jesus brings power and passion together. The covenant of God with his people, made on Sinai and affirmed throughout the Old Testament, brings together the power of the creating God with the yearning love of the liberating God. The heart of the Old Testament – perhaps the key discovery made by the Israelites in their Babylonian exile – was that the creator God and the liberator God were one and the same. The God who had acted in the exodus to set Israel free from slavery acted with the power of the God who had made the heavens and the earth. Both actions were for a single purpose – to make a people to be in relationship with him – and for that same purpose he would act again to bring the exile to an end. And that definitive action, bringing exile to an end, is Jesus' resurrection: victory over death, subversion of the Jerusalem authorities, and overthrow of the might of Rome – the complete expression of the power and the passion of God.

And this leaves us with the gospel, the mission of Mary Magdalene to share this good news with friends, enemies, and strangers. This gospel is the politics of power and passion – the politics of Jesus. It is time to summarize this gospel in conclusion.

THE POLITICS OF POWER AND PASSION

The argument of this book has been that Jesus invites a new kind of passion because he brings a new kind of power. Let me take that argument in gradual stages.

We observed the old kind of passion in a variety of forms. Most attractively, in Mary Magdalene, it was a lament, a simple, doleful gesture like laying flowers by the roadside after a road traffic accident. It said, if it cannot be happy, make it beautiful. We also saw Peter's passion, with all its flaws – founded on his own strength, with an attitude of superiority toward the other disciples, and convinced that he knows better than Jesus. We speculated about the passion of Mrs Pilate, locked up inside the need for her to play a role as the wife of the governor that she may have found to be a prison, a passion that dares not speak its incipient faith. We saw the suppressed passion of Joseph of Arimathaea and Nicodemus, with aspects of Mary Magdalene's beautiful gestures about it, but with the determination to keep its faith to the nighttime and a reluctance to let its passion interfere with its power – the power of being a member of the Sanhedrin. We saw Barabbas's passion, the passion for purity and change, a passion all too contemporary in the life of members of al-Qaeda today. And we failed to discern Pontius Pilate's passion – only discovering how determined he was to prevent a discussion of the truth.

The old kind of power is the controlling force governing this constrained form of passion. Pilate embodies this notion of power – public office, patronage, property, and wealth, all backed up by the ready threat of military coercion. Barabbas almost entirely shares Pilate's notion of power; that is why Barabbas's revolution would not seriously change anything. Nicodemus and Joseph begin to see that the passion brought by Jesus may offer a different kind of power – but their lives are deeply invested in the power represented by Pilate, and they do not let Jesus shape their decisive commitments. Mrs Pilate we know little about, but we have assumed that her whole social, economic, and domestic well-being depends on accepting her husband's understanding of and practice of power. Peter assumes the power of Pilate even in the presence of Jesus – hence his horror of the cross and his attack on the servant of the high priest. He falls back on his own power at his moment of crisis in the courtyard. But at the lakeshore he discovers a new kind of power. The woman at Bethany displays something of this power, and Mary Magdalene discovers a new power in the garden.

The new kind of power is the power of resurrection. In the last two chapters we have explored some of the dimensions of this new power. This indeed is a power beyond description. It is not subdued by death. It has the force of a new creation, a significance as great as God's original purpose for the world. It therefore cannot be subjugated by military coercion or crippling taxation or monopolized patronage or arbitrary violence. It is the power of God's desire for his people, the power of unquenchable longing and deep patience. It is the power of encounter between God and his people, as dynamic as the experience of Israel in receiving and treasuring the Law bestowed at Mount Sinai and kept in the first Jerusalem temple. It is not subdued by sin. Even the most harrowing betrayal is met with challenge, companionship, and transformation – Peter is changed from a shamefaced sinner to a commissioned leader in one short conversation. It is no longer frightened of the past, because the power of forgiveness makes even terrible mistakes redeemable and opens gateways to new possibilities. And it is founded on friendship – the friendship between God and his people, embodied in the breaking of bread together – and it offers a living experience of new power for the world. None of these features of the new power are ones the old power can comprehend.

The new kind of passion is made possible by the new kind of power. No longer is passion simply an erotic or idealistic distraction from politics; no longer is it a cultivation of self or sentimentality in the face of the realities of sin and suffering. In the light of the power of the resurrection, passion is now any and every intimation or reflection of the yearning love of God for his people and his longing to restore relationship with them, even if it means the cross. This passion is patient, because it waits as longs as God does. It is sometimes painful, as we speculated it may have been for Mrs Pilate when she said, "I have suffered a great deal today in a dream because of him." It is tender in the way that the anointing at Bethany was tender. It is persistent in the way that Mary Magdalene's vigil at cross and tomb was persistent. It is never ending, as Mary Magdalene's search for Jesus – reflecting the woman's search in the Song of Songs – is never ending. It is invariably in the home of the sick and in the company of the poor, as we saw in Bethany. And it is on a cosmic scale, as it consciously or unconsciously displays the fundamental pouring out of God's love and restoration of friendship. It is a passion as crazy as the crazy heart of God.

I call this "the politics of power and passion" because it highlights that the new power and the new passion have a truly social significance. These are not simply personal things (even if one accepts the notion that there are "simply personal things"). The old power assumed that certain things were given – most of all death – and that what mattered was who controlled the maximum number of resources, especially those that were publicly accountable (such as taxation and, in a different sense, law), and who enforced compliance via coercion to the point of death. Passion in this context is just window dressing – a distraction from the serious business of politics, which is about the negotiation and manipulation of power. But into this situation comes the resurrection of Jesus Christ, the overturning of the power of death. No longer therefore can coercion to the point of death maintain a stranglehold on power; there is here a greater power. No longer can the distribution of scarce resources be the characteristic nature of politics. Politics becomes the reorientation of life according to the freedom made possible by the power of overcoming death, and not just death but sin – through the power of forgiveness. Thus those aspects of society that had previously been just window dressing – lament in the face of death, bitterness and regret in the face of sin, in short, passion – now become the key points of transformation, the nerve centers of the new politics. We still need laws, and we still need taxes, but the control of these things is no longer the definition of politics; politics is the reordering of passion in line with a new order of power. Now, in the resurrection of Jesus, we can see that every small gesture of reconciliation or care of the vulnerable is part of the way God is transforming the world. Power and passion come together at last.

OPPORTUNITIES FOR INDIVIDUAL
OR GROUP REFLECTION

I wonder what it is like to know that someone you deeply care about is going to die and there is nothing you can do about it.

I wonder what it is like to see expensive materials wasted.

I wonder whether there is a shortage of the things that really matter.

I wonder what is the best way to commemorate a violent death.

I wonder what it is like to search and search but not really to hope that you will ever find.

I wonder what it is like to see but not to believe.

I wonder what it might be like to discover that one's passion was always, more or less, a passion for God.

I wonder what it is to discover the greatest power in the universe.

I wonder what difference that greatest power might make to our assumptions and expectations of life.

I wonder what you could do if you didn't mind who got the credit.

I wonder what it might be like not to need to run away from anything in the past.

I wonder what it would be like not to fear death.

God of power and passion,
whose Son, Jesus Christ, was anointed for burial and laid
    in the tomb
yet rose and met your servant Mary in the garden:
renew us in the way we touch one another,
that our passion may be offered as gentleness,
our desire as kindness,
and our longing as a beautiful sign of your longing for us;
be close to and heal those for whom human touch
has been experienced as hurt, shame, and abuse;
and let our gestures of extravagance and compassion
always be directed, like yours,
toward the poor, the outcast, and the notorious sinner.

Make us a people whose hope lies in your politics,
whose heart lies in your passion,
and whose power lies in your resurrection,
so that our life together in you may offer your world
your new creation, your desire for us,
your forgiveness, and your good news.

Move us from lives lost in lament and obsessed by control
to a patient, tender, persistent, never ending, cosmic passion
that reorders power in the spirit of the resurrection of your
    Son, Jesus Christ. Amen.

A NOTE ON SOURCES
AND FURTHER READING

The book that inspired this one was John Howard Yoder, *The Politics of Jesus: Vicit Agnus Noster*, second edition (Grand Rapids, MI: Eerdmans, 1994). Yoder more than anyone helped me see that the issues that faced Jesus are the issues that face us and that his way should be our way. Perhaps my next major source of insight was Ched Myers, *Binding the Strong Man: A Political Reading of Mark's Story of Jesus* (Maryknoll, NY: Orbis, 1988).

The book I turned to most frequently was Wes Howard-Brook, *Becoming Children of God: John's Gospel and Radical Discipleship* (Eugene, OR: Wipf and Stock, 2003), which together with Mark Stibbe, *John* (London and New York: Sheffield Academic Press, 1996) has transformed my understanding of John's gospel. A constant source of encouragement and wisdom was Frederick Dale Bruner, *Matthew: A Commentary – Volume One: The Christbook, Matthew 1–12* and *Matthew: A Commentary – Volume Two: The Churchbook, Matthew 13–28*, revised and expanded editions (Grand Rapids, MI: Eerdmans, 2004). Another consistently rewarding resource was Raymond E. Brown, *The Death of the Messiah: From Gethsemane to the Grave*, two volumes (New

York: Doubleday, 1994). Also significant in shaping the approach, particularly to the first chapter, was Warren Carter, *Pontius Pilate: Portraits of a Roman Governor* (Collegeville, MN: Liturgical, 2003). The practice of wondering I learned (along with much else) from the great children's catechist Jerome Berryman. See particularly his *The Complete Guide to Godly Play, Volume One: How to Lead Godly Play Lessons* (Denver, CO: Living the Good News, 2002). If you have enjoyed this book, these are all books that would deepen your knowledge and understanding.

Of the studies for a more specialist readership, the following have been particularly helpful. Helen K. Bond, *Pontius Pilate in History and Interpretation* (Cambridge and New York: Cambridge Univ. Press, 1998); Martin Hengel, *The Zealots: Investigations into the Jewish Freedom Movement in the Period from Herod I until 70 A.D.*, translated by David W. Smith (Edinburgh: T & T Clark, 1989); Bruce D. Winter, *Roman Wives, Roman Widows: The Appearance of New Women and the Pauline Communities* (Grand Rapids, MI: Eerdmans, 2003); Shaul K. Bar, *Dreams in the Bible* (PhD dissertation, New York Univ., 1987); Elisabeth Schussler Fiorenza, *In Memory of Her: A Feminist Theological Construction of Christian Origins* (New York: Herder and Herder, 1994); Saba Mahmood, *Politics of Piety: The Islamic Revival and the Feminist Subject* (Princeton, NJ: Princeton Univ. Press, 2005). I am also grateful to Stanley Hauerwas for an unpublished essay, "Sacrificing the Sacrifices of War", which provided me with the stories and some of the reasoning behind the section on sacrifice in chapter 2. The stories of soldiers' experiences come from Lt. Col. Dave Grossman, *On Killing: The Psychological Cost of Learning to Kill in War and Society* (Boston: Little Brown and Company, 1995).

Those who may wish to pursue how I have developed themes raised here in my other writing may choose to look at *Improvisation and the Drama of Christian Ethics* (Grand Rapids, MI: Brazos and London: SPCK, 2004), which considers how apparently powerless people may nonetheless exert influence while remaining faithful, and *God's Companions: Reimagining Christian Ethics* (Oxford and Malden, MA: Blackwell, 2006), which considers the way Christians practice abundance rather than scarcity.

NOTES

1. John Howard Yoder, *The Politics of Jesus*, 2nd ed. (Grand Rapids: Eerdmans, 1994), 39.

2. Wes Howard-Brook, *Becoming Children of God: John's Gospel and Radical Discipleship* (Eugene, OR: Wipf and Stock, 2003), 29.

3. Howard-Brook, *Becoming the Children of God*, 189.

4. Mark W. G. Stibbe, *John* (London and New York: Sheffield Academic Press, 1996), 182, 184.

5. Ched Myers, *Binding the Strong Man: A Political Reading of Mark's Story of Jesus* (Maryknoll, NY: Orbis, 1988), 280–81.

6. Mark W. G. Stibbe, *John* (London and New York: Sheffield Academic Press, 1996), 201.